Who Controls America?

Mark Mullen

Who Controls America?

Names: Mullen, Mark, 1954-

Title: Who controls America? / Mark Mullen.

Description: First edition. | Haddon Township, NJ : Mark Mullen, [2017] | Includes bibliographical references.

Identifiers: LCCN 2017906611 | ISBN 978-0-692-87694-7

Subjects: LCSH: Power (Social sciences)--United States--History--21st century. | United States--Politics and government--21st century. | Banks and banking, Central--United States--History--21st century. | Wall Street (New York, N.Y.)--History--21st century. | United States--Foreign relations--21st century.

Classification: LCC HN90.P6 M85 2017 | DDC 303.30973--dc23

Printed in the United States of America

First Edition

Contents

INTRODUCTION

"Elites, not masses, govern America. In an industrial, scientific, and nuclear age, life in a democracy, just as in a totalitarian society, is shaped by a handful of men. In spite of differences in their approach to the study of power in America, scholars— political scientists and sociologists alike— agree that 'the key political, economic, and social decisions are made by tiny minorities." Irony of Democracy, Thomas R. Dye, L. Harmon Zeigler

America is a wonderful place to live and grow old for a majority of the masses. We have many freedoms and opportunities for work, recreation, worship, travel, and just plain leisure. We can criticize our government openly without fear of a midnight home invasion by government warriors. We worship at any church of our choosing. Some even choose not to worship, and that is okay. Americans enjoy many comforts and opportunities that other nations can only dream of. But is America functioning as the country we need it to be? The country it can be? No country will ever be perfect or meet the needs of all its citizens, but are we moving in the right direction?

Introduction

Recent indicators seem to show that America is going in the wrong direction.

A 2014 Gallup poll found that Americans were less satisfied with their level of freedoms than at any other time in modern history. In fact, the United States ranked number 36 out of 120 countries surveyed. But what do we mean by freedoms? Gallup concluded that for Americans, freedom is associated with the economy. When the economy is down, or lacking confidence, Americans perceive an erosion of freedoms due to less household money available to spend on leisure activities. But who controls the economy? Would you believe it is a singular private organization supported by the U.S, Department of Treasury and the Congress? You better believe it because it is true. This one group has created massive wealth for a few while inflicting huge debt and taxes (in the form of inflation) on the middle class.

The economy is not the only issue bringing heartburn to Americans. According to Gallup, roughly 75 percent of Americans believe their government to be corrupt.[1] This includes Congress, the Supreme Court, and the presidency. Political corruption contributes to a sense of reduced freedoms due to bad policies and regulations that interfere with personal choice making. But corruption takes more than one player. Large scale corruption requires large scale resources. And there is a group, a small body of organizations that possess the resources to control Washington. And they do.

A national survey conducted by The Center for the New American Dream found that "80 percent of Americans believe that it is more difficult to achieve the American Dream than it was 10 years ago. The number was 64 percent in 2004."[2] One of the reasons preventing Americans from realizing that dream is education. Did you know that only about 35 percent of American fourth-graders are proficient in reading? That's because colleges do not teach prospective teachers how to teach reading. When children can't read by the end of third grade, they're unlikely to ever read beyond a very basic early childhood level. That is why more than 8,000 students quit high school every day, limiting their lifetime earning potential and putting a strain on welfare related services.[3] The sad part of this is a few university elites planned for this result. And Congress helped them. Together, they don't want smart kids. Actually, they don't want smart adults.

The elites control every aspect of higher education from tuition to the curriculum in order to limit both enrollment and access to the opportunities afforded by a college education. Want proof? Ask yourself if a college degree is still the ticket to the career of your choice, better pay, and a sustainable middles class lifestyle. If it was, the middle class would be increasing in size and wealth rather than decreasing. Do you suffer from sticker shock when you see the cost of tuition? You should. Did you know that the annual cost of tuition for a state college in 1971 was $428? Today, tuition for one year at a state college is $9,139. That is a 2,035 percent increase over 46 years. Meanwhile, the median household income for an American family in 1971 was $9,030. For 2015 (latest data available at publication), the median household income was $55,775. That is a 515 percent increase. If tuition rose in lock step with median household income, tuition at a state college in 2017 would be about $2,200 per year. And if income kept pace with tuition costs, the 2016 annual median household income would have been $183,862. Did your household earn $184,000 during 2016? Still think Congress wants everyone to go to college?

The world appears to be a much more dangerous place than it has ever been. Unfortunately, for the last 100 years, but especially since the 1960s, our foreign policies have been led by single-minded ideologues who believed they could manipulation world events like a puppet master controls a marionette. And like Geppetto's Pinocchio, America's foreign policy laughed in the face of its creators. Rather than building a better and friendlier world, our foreign policies have bolstered global terrorism, increased rouge nation bad behaviors, and made skeptics out of friends.

Both Americans and the rest of the world are dissatisfied with our place in global affairs. Polls and surveys continue to show that a majority of Americans, and the world, are unhappy with the way America interacts with the world community. Of course, the National Security Agency surveillance program on friendly nations didn't help matters.

CHAPTER 1. The Federal Banking System

"Inflation is made in one place and one place only, Washington, D.C. In Washington, D.C. the chief source of inflation is a Greek temple on Constitution Avenue which houses the Federal Reserve Board." - Milton Friedman

From America's very beginning, citizens relied on paper currency as a means for trade. Early colonists had no other choice as gold and silver mines had not yet been discovered within the boundaries of the United States. Bank notes, not gold, drove America's fledging economy. Not much has changed in nearly 270 years. Banks still wield significant influence over the direction of the economy.

Banks are important to our economy because they serve as the middleman between providers and users of goods and services. They contribute to the economy in four basic ways:

1. They serve as a safe place for people and corporations to park their money for future use. Banks pay savers a fee, or interest, for the privilege of being the garage that stores your money. Interest provides the saver with

additional income to spend on goods and services.

2. Banks move money from buyers to sellers. Online purchasing of goods and services would not be possible if not for electronic transfers of cash by banks.

3. Banks issue mortgages and personal loans that can be used to purchase expensive items such as a home, car, or for the expansion of business.

4. Banks earn money several ways. First, they loan bank deposits from savers to borrowers at an interest rate high enough to provide a positive return to the savers while covering all banking costs. Secondly, banks issue credit cards to individuals and businesses. The credit cards provide us with instant cash value which is used to purchase goods and services. In return for handling this transaction, the bank charges both the user and the merchant a fee, or interest, for using the credit.

Banks, especially the federal government banking systems, have played a significant role in creating the sour economic conditions in today's America. Let's examine how America's biggest bank, the federal government, influences economic activity. But first, we need to identify all the moving parts of the federal government banking system.

We begin with the many credit granting arms of the federal government. For starters, a few of the well-known include:

- Federal Deposit Insurance Corporation, or FDIC
- Federal Housing Administration, or FHA
- The Small Business Administration, or SBA
- United States Department of Agriculture, or USDA
- U.S. Department of Housing and Urban Development, or HUD
- Federal Stafford Loans
- Troubled Asset Relief Program, or TARP

These are just a few of the federal government's 120 different programs spread throughout 30 agencies. And let's not forget to mention the eleven banks sponsored by the federal government that support housing projects. These banks are known as the Federal Home Loan Banks and have existed since 1932. Lest we forget, the federal government also controls Freddie Mac and Fannie Mae.

Federal credit programs are designed to finance those individuals considered to be high risk for default, such as an 18-year-old college student or a low-wage home buyer. These banking arms of the federal government provide the American public with financial assistance to homeowners and businesses in a declared disaster area, to house farm laborers, for the purchase of houses, education, small business and other farm subsidies. At the close of the 2015 fiscal year, the federal government held over $10 trillion in loans and guarantees with its credit programs. [4]

These federal credit programs add up to a mountain of federal debt – over $3 trillion. High government debt slows economic growth. Slow economic growth depresses worker wages. Low wages translates into lost opportunities to purchase new goods and services. Less consumption of products and services curbs job creation.

But perhaps the most well-known and influential arm of the federal banking system is the Federal Reserve System, commonly known as the Fed or Federal Reserve. The Fed controls the Federal funds rate, also known as the overnight interest rate. The overnight interest rate is the rate that large banks use when borrowing and lending money from one another in the overnight market. (This is dependent on the number and amount of each day's financial transactions, a bank may need to borrow money overnight to ensure it has enough cash on hand to meet the reserve requirements mandated by the Federal Reserve.)

The Federal funds rate is affected by the Discount Rate, the rate the federal government charges banks if they decide to borrow directly from the Fed. Since the Fed would rather that banks borrow from each other, they usually keep the Discount Rate 0.5 to one percent higher than the Federal Funds.

The stated purpose of Federal funds rate manipulation is to generate long-term economic stability and growth. When times are tough with economic slowdowns, the Fed lowers the Federal Funds Rate with the intent that small businesses and giant corporations will borrow more money to generate an upswing in the production and sale of goods and services. High Federal funds rates are used when the money supply climbs higher than desired levels. This move discourages banks from lending money to each other and businesses to keep bank reserves at or above the Fed minimum deposit level.

Unfortunately for the American middle class, Fed manipulation of interest rates almost always fails to deliver economic growth or stability. Why? Well, the Fed does not actually create anything, not a single good, service, or job. What the Fed does by manipulating interest rates is no more than the pea-in-the-shell magic trick. The Fed simply transfers wealth from savers to borrowers or from borrowers to savers. No new wealth is created, it is just shifted from one shell to another. Relocating wealth from one sector to another does not produce long-term economic growth.

A Brief History of the Fed and Its Influence on the Economy

The Fed was created under the Federal Reserve Act of 1913. Its sole purpose was to provide bank liquidity through security loans to banks that were suffering from runs on deposit withdrawals by customers, such as the ones of 1893 and 1907. In both waves of panic, Wall Street bailed out the federal government with sizable loans. In 1910 a Washington senator and a few Wall Street bankers came together for a secret meeting at Jekyll Island, Georgia in search of a better way to ward off future bank runs. The plan they developed became the foundation for the Federal Reserve System. The Fed would consist of twelve central banks regulating America's banking industry.

A secondary, but important, idea behind the creation of the Fed was to dethrone Wall Street bankers as rulers of America's economy through regulations. But it did not work. In his book *Americas Sixty Families*, Ferdinand Lundberg writes, *"In practice, the Federal Reserve Bank of New York became the fountainhead of the system of twelve regional banks, for New York was the money market of the nation. The other eleven banks were so many expensive mausoleums erected to salve the local pride and quell the Jacksonian fears of the hinterland."*[5]

The reason the Federal Reserve Bank of New York become dominant was that it was governed by a wealthy and powerful Wall Street banker, Benjamin Strong. In addition to being the first Governor of the Federal Reserve Bank of New York, Strong was also president of J.P. Morgan's Bankers Trust Company of New York. As you might have suspected, Strong manipulated the Fed at the discretion of executives representing the leading New York banks.

The importance of the Federal Reserve Bank of New York cannot be underscored. From the beginning, its tentacles reached out across the world to protect Wall Street banks. For example, during World War I, Midwestern farms had banner crop yields and soaring profits. As you would expect, the farmers deposited their profits with local banks. They invested some in war bonds but did not participate in the stock market. Their money did not make it to New York institutions. This was unbearable to Wall Street bankers as they were experiencing declining deposits during this time. New York wanted the money to come east. And they found an underhanded way to do it. They used the Fed.

The plan used by the Fed under the direction of the Federal Reserve Bank of New York was simple, devious, and destructive for Midwestern farmers, their local banks, and America. The Fed would provide local banks with low-interest money targeted for farmers through the newly created Federal Farm Loan Board. The plan was to entice farmers to borrow cheap money to purchase farm equipment, build new barns, and purchase more land. Then, at a later point in time, the Fed would create a recession to lower crop profits and force farmers into bankruptcy. And that is what they did.

In May 1920, the Fed held a secret meeting and made the decision to dramatically tighten credit by raising interest rates from 4.74 percent to six percent. One month later, the Fed raised interest rates to seven percent and kept it there until May 1921. This put the country in a recession while wiping out many farmers, local banks, and destroying the lives of millions of Americans. In his book *The Economic Pinch*, Charles A. Lindbergh, Sr. wrote, *"This contraction of credit and currency had the effect, the next year, of diminishing the national production $15,000,000,000; it had the effect of throwing millions of people out of employment; it had the effect of reducing the value of lands and ranches $20,000,000,000."*[6] Lindbergh also went on to say, *"Under the Federal Reserve Act, panics are scientifically created; the present panic is the first scientifically created one, worked out as we figure a mathematical problem."*

Proof of Lindbergh's findings is evident in how the Fed treated city banks versus rural banks. The

Fed extended credit to city banks during the summer of 1920 to allow them to offer credit to industry, wholesalers, and retailers permitting these banks to survive. Country banks received no help from the Fed and were told to collect debts owed by growers crushing farmers and small banks.

The Federal Reserve Bank of New York received some help from the United States Congress in pulling off its scheme of putting farmers out of business while sending their money to New York banks. In 1920, Congress approved the Esch-Cummins Railroad Act. This new law granted the Interstate Commerce Commission the power to fix rates charged by the railroads. Esch-Cummins returned the railroads to private ownership and guaranteed owners a profit for the first six months of operation. (The federal government took over control of railroads during WWI.) This new law contributed to the destruction of farmers because the same people who owned the big New York banks also owned the railroads. Here's how it hurt the farmers.

During World War I, the U.S. Treasury sold Liberty Bonds to finance the war. All American citizens were encouraged to borrow money to support their country through the purchase of these bonds. And they did. About $17 billion were bought. Because the New York bankers owned the railroads and wanted the wealth that the agriculture industry had accumulated prior to and during WWI, they used the Esch-Cummins Act as a weapon to acquire the farmer's money. Rail rates were set unreasonably high making it more expensive and less profitable for the farmer to get his product to market. *"In many cases transportation charges will exceed the price paid the farmer."*[7] High transportation rates combined with banks demanding repayment of all loans forced the farmers to do the unthinkable, the selling of their Liberty Bonds. Conveniently, New York bankers were ready and waiting to help the farmers through this difficult time by purchasing their bonds. The bankers paid eighty-five cents on the dollar to the farmer and then resold the bonds for one hundred cents on the dollar. Adding insult to injury, the farmer not only lost fifteen cents per Liberty Bond share, but he was also indebted to repay the interest on the loan used for the original purchase of the bonds.

The recession of 1920-21 was created by the Fed doing exactly the opposite of what it was designed to do. It created a run on small country banks and a lack of national economic stability. Deflation between May 1920 and July 1921 has been estimated to be in the range between 14 to 18 percent – the highest amount since 1780. Commodity prices collapsed by over 100 percent. Wholesale prices fell by over 36 percent. Unemployment rose from five percent to over 11 percent. Stocks declined by 47 percent while it is estimated that business failures rose by 225 percent. Surviving businesses saw earnings decline by 75 percent.

After the recession of 1920-21, the Fed bounced rates up and down several times. Then in 1924, the Fed decided to create $500 million in new credit. There were two reasons for the credit expansion. The first was to boost a declining business climate in America. The second reason was to support the Bank of England in an effort to restore pre-WWI exchange rates and pull England out of depression. By weakening the value of the dollar relative to the British pound, gold reserves would move from America to England. And why would the Fed care about another nation's economy? New York bankers had loaned billions of dollars to England during WWI. A depressed English economy would be hard-pressed making repayments. That would be bad for New York banks. The Fed, run by Wall Street bankers, could not let that happen.

The unexpected and welcomed (by bankers) consequence of a surplus of cheap credit was the average citizen's interest in purchasing stocks. Having purchased Liberty Bonds to support the war effort, Americans were becoming more comfortable with investing in security instruments. And with low-interest rates and credit easily available, banks encouraged average Americans to invest in the stock market using borrowed money and margin purchases. Buying on margin allows investors to buy more shares of stock because the investors need only pay 10 percent of the share purchase price. The remaining 90 percent of share value is borrowed and repaid when the investor sells the stock, hopefully for a profit. When applying the margin formula, an average person with $100 could buy $1,000 worth of stock. The Fed was aware of both the speculative application of borrowed money and the euphoric enjoyment experienced by the average American as they invested and made money in the stock market. The Fed consciously used that knowledge to manipulate public behavior (borrow and buy) at the request of the New York bankers rather than to set sound monetary policy.

By the mid-1920s, over three million Americans were invested in the stock market. By the late 1920s, 40 percent of every dollar loaned was to purchase stock. And by September 1929, stock prices had risen by 400 percent per average share between 1923 and 1929.[8] This rise was mainly due to speculative buying of stocks on credit. The higher stock prices rose, the more people borrowed to purchase new shares. The buying frenzy on speculative purchases, however, did not reflect real potential earnings per share price. Eventually, something has to give, and it did on Black Tuesday 1929.

Beginning in September 1929, stock prices began falling and kept falling until the market crashed on Tuesday, October 29, 1929. Different economists have varied opinions as to what caused the Great Depression, but there can be no question that the Fed was the prime mover of the crash and the following depression. *"In November 1923, the Federal Reserve began increasing its holdings in government securities (such as Treasury bonds) by a factor of six, from $73 million to $477 million. This keeps rates low, not by setting them explicitly but by forcing the price of bonds up, which has the net effect of driving rates down."*9 This time prior to the crash was often referred to as the Roaring Twenties.

Prior to the crash in October 1929, the Fed announced it was going to contract the money supply by raising the discount rate to six percent. This action increased the rate that banks paid to borrow funds from the Federal Reserve, thus raising the rates paid by all borrowers. Even as banks were asking customers to repay loans, the president of the National City Bank (the largest bank in New York) who also happened to be a director of Federal Reserve Bank of New York continued to urge Americans to purchase stocks.

With tight credit and loans due, investors began selling off stocks to stay afloat. As sellers outnumbered buyers, stock prices sank, and the market crashed. But there is more to the Great Depression than the collapse of the stock market.

As investors cashed out of the market, some deposited what little funds they had back into their local bank. Others withdrew all funds from the bank. This had a negative effect on the banks because as deposits grew, the Fed's reserve requirements grew in lock-step with deposits. When reserves declined, banks were forced to purchase loans from other banks to increase their assets. This yo-yo effect put additional financial stress on banks as they often fell temporarily short of reserves forcing some banks to close their doors before closing time on days of heavy withdrawals.

Americans noticed. Many average Americans lost their life savings in the crash and gained a distrust of banks. Their desire to purchase anything that was not an absolute necessity and could not be paid for in cash disappeared. As a result, manufacturing declined, commerce slowed to a halt, and unemployment began to rise quickly. The money supply contracted even more than planned by the Fed.

By the end of 1930 small, Midwestern banks were running out of money. They needed an infusion of credit from the Fed. They didn't get it as the Fed was only focused on the financial health of the big New York banks. Small banks began closing their doors for good – nearly 750 during the first ten months of 1930. But the Fed overestimated the strength of the big banks and on December 11, 1930, allowed the Bank of the United States the fourth largest in New York City, to crash. Its collapse wiped out the accounts of an estimated 400,000 depositors along with $200 million. (The Bank of the United States was created in 1913 and was not considered to be a power bank as it catered to the average citizen rather than corporations and wealthy individuals.) By the end of 1933 Americans had lost roughly $140 billion through bank failures. Only after Franklin D. Roosevelt declared a bank holiday, closing all banks from March 6, 1933 to March 10, 1933, and asked Congress to pass Emergency Banking Act, did the run on banks subside.

The Fed was created to prevent bank panics, so what happened? Let's start with the Fed's flawed policy. Between 1929 and 1932, the Fed shrunk the amount of money in the economy by one-third causing the recession of late 1929 to turn into a full blown multi-year depression. Shrinking the quantity of money in the economy created deflation which increased debt. Mounting debts caused reduced consumption of products and increased unemployment. High unemployment led to bankrupt businesses, banks, and individuals.

Instead of contracting the monetary base the Fed should have been expanding it in order to save banks and stem deflation. They didn't because, like most government agencies, the governors of the Fed could not agree on a course of action, so they did nothing. Failure to act was the wrong action.

The Fed was not the only government entity that created the Great Depression. It had help from Congress and President Hoover.

In the summer of 1930, Congress passed the Smoot-Hawley Tariff Act raising American tariffs on imports by some 20 percent. The rest of the world did not like this and reacted in kind. American exports fell from over $5 billion in 1929 to roughly $1.5 billion in 1932. Unemployment in export industries exploded and farmers who normally exported nearly a quarter of wheat production and half of all cotton and tobacco saw their markets totally collapse.

As if Americans weren't already down and out, President Hoover and Congress landed another devastating blow to the American people. Hoover signed into law the Revenue Act of 1932 which doubled the income tax for American workers. Corporation taxes were raised by 15 percent, and the estate tax was doubled. Under the act, new taxes were also imposed. There was the gift tax ranging from 0.75 to 33.74 percent, a 10 percent gasoline tax, a three percent automobile tax, a telephone usage tax, a 0.2 cents check tax, and postal rates increased from 0.2 cents to 0.3 cents for a first-class letter.

After Roosevelt's bank holiday, the economy began to recover, and the Fed remained relatively passive over the next few years. That is until the summer of 1936 and spring of 1937. The Fed was concerned that banks were holding more money in reserves than required by law. (The banks had learned from past panics and bank closures. They had increased their reserves to protect themselves against a future bank run.) Consequentially, if inflation were to return the Fed would have a difficult time tightening the money supply when banks already had a surplus. So the Fed took action. It raised bank reserve requirements three times, August 1936, March 1937, and May 1937 doubling reserve requirements. Unfortunately for the American people, these steps reduced the amount of money available for commercial and business loans and sent the United States into a 13-month recession. Unemployment rose to 19 percent, GDP fell 10 percent, and manufacturing fell by 32 percent.

Throughout the early to mid-1940s, the Fed focused its energies on the war efforts, mostly by purchasing government bonds. It did nothing extreme to hurt the economy. For the remainder of the 1940s and most of the 1950s, the Fed continued its focus on purchasing Treasury bonds and took no actions that had an adverse effect on the economy. However, the U.S. economy went into a steep recession lasting 10 months from August 1957 to April 1958. Like the previous recessions, most economists believe the Fed caused this one by slowing economic growth to prevent inflation. The Fed erroneously raised the Fed funds rate decreasing money supply while increasing interest rates on borrowed money.

The United States entered the 1960s with an unemployment rate of 7.1 percent and less than full manufacturing capacity output. For the most part, these were just part of the business cycle of an economy still recovering from the Korean War. It was the mid-1960s when things get interesting once again. It was the beginning of an inflationary era that lasted through the early 1980s. Here's what happened.

By 1965 the Kennedy-Johnson across-the-board tax cuts of 1964 and the escalation of the Vietnam War led to maximum industrial production – demand for products outpaced manufacturing capacity. The result was rising prices. Then factor in the government's cost of Vietnam (12 percent of the federal budget) and the price tag of Lyndon Johnson's new program, the Great Society (Medicare and Medicaid) and you have soaring inflation and rising government debt. (You can't pay for a war and new expensive social programs by cutting revenue.)

To combat this inflation, the Fed raised the Fed funds rate multiple times from January 1, 1966 to November 1966, from 3.90 to 5.76 percent. A tightening money supply meant a tightening in credit and less money for business to build manufacturing capacity and inventory to meet demand. Prices stayed high. The Feds contracting of credit only served to increase inflation from 1.7 percent in November 1965 to 3.6 percent in November 1966. So the Fed began lowering the Fed funds rate in January 1967. Milton Friedman, a Nobel Prize-winning economist, referred to this *"as the beginning of an extended departure from price stability, an inflation roller-coaster around a rising trend, with the occasional deviations below that trend reflecting shifts to monetary restraint that were abandoned once recessions developed."*[10]

The use of this stop-go monetary policy by the Fed led to two recessions in the 1970s. (The stop-go policy was the Feds way of alternating the fight between high unemployment and high inflation. The Fed viewed unemployment and inflation as incompatible problems.) The first, in 1970, was rather mild and lasted for 11 months. It was the second recession that was crippling. Lasting from November 1973 to March 1975, the Fed funds rate skyrocketed to 13 percent, inflation grew to 12 percent, the price of oil quadrupled creating gas shortages at the pumps, and Richard Nixon instituted wage-price controls. These actions combined kept consumer good prices high which reduced demand and forced unemployment up to nine percent. It seemed that unemployment and inflation were not contrary but joined at the hip and grew together making the stop-go policy useless.

With inflation still at 10 percent, the Fed doubled the Fed funds rate from 10.25 percent to 20 percent in March 1980. The Fed kept this rate until May 1981. It ended inflation but created another recession lasting from July 1981 until November 1982. Not just another ordinary recession but the worst one since 1929. Unemployment hit 11 percent overall. In manufacturing, unemployment was the cruelest with 75 percent of all job losses coming in the manufacturing industries. Crop prices fell, and corporate bankruptcies increased over 50 percent from 1981.

Economic stability in the 1980s came slowly. Although inflation remained at five percent between 1983 and 1987, the U.S. trade deficit was $150 billion, the federal budget deficit was $220 billion, and the stock market crashed on October 19, 1987. In fact, it was the largest one-day market crash in history with the DOW losing 22.6 percent of its value. But unlike 1929, the market recovered within days. But it wasn't until year's end 1987 that job growth finally took hold and produced an unemployment rate of under six percent.

But not all was going in the right direction during the mid-to-late 1980s. Savings and Loans institutions were silently suffering. S&Ls could not pay depositors high enough interest rates to fend off a new competitor for savers – money market accounts. The federal government set the interest rates that S&Ls could pay on deposits, and those rates were substantially less than what could be earned in market accounts. As a result, S&Ls began collapsing. By 1989, one-thousand had failed. The Savings and Loans Crises saw the greatest number of bank closings since the Great Depression. In August 1989 Congress passed the Financial Institutions Reform, Recovery, and Enforcement Act of 1989. The legislation provided $50 billion to close failed banks and stem further losses and to regulate the industry better. In the following six years, the government shut down approximately an additional 750 S&Ls holding $400 billion in assets.

The Savings and Loan Crises of 1989 set the table for another recession lasting from July 1990 through March 1991. Once again, the Fed had a hand in creating this recession. From December 1988 through April 1991 credit was kept tight to lower the rate of inflation. It only succeeded in slowing down the economy. After the Fed lowered the Fed funds rate in April, the economy began a slow recovery. For the remainder of the 1990s, inflation remained at a fairly constant rate of three percent – a value lower than the 70s and 80s but higher than the 50s and 60s.

The turn of the century brought a mild recession in November 2001. However, the September 11, 2001, terrorist's attacks on New York and Washington D.C. most likely helped to turn a cyclical business slowdown into a recession. Economic expansion had begun to slow in March 2001, but the attacks shut down the economy for days, seriously reduced airline travel, and raised concerns among Americans about our way of life going forward.

From 2001 through 2007 the U.S. economy expanded, albeit much weaker than previous post-recession expansions. Employment grew at an anemic pace of 0.9 percent, salaries grew at a feeble 1.8 percent, and GDP growth was a shabby 2.7 percent. But nevertheless, the economy was moving in the right direction until 2008 when the Great Recession began. And once again, the Fed triggered a financial crises which brought America to its knees.

In began in the summer of 2004 with the Fed raising the Fed funds rate due to fear that housing prices had become over-inflated. By December 2005, the Fed funds rate was 4.25 percent. This moved the interest rates on a two-year Treasury note to 4.40

percent. However, the interest rate on a seven-year Treasury note was only 4.39 percent. When the yield on a short-term note becomes greater than the yield of a long-term note the phenomenon is known as an inverted yield curve. Economists view an inverted yield curve as a prime indicator of an impending economic recession. The Fed chose to ignore this warning and continued to raise the Fed funds rate even though the inverted yield curve grew larger by each passing month. By July 2006 the interest rate on a three-month note was 5.11 percent while interest on a 10-year bill was 5.06 percent. This disparity between short-term and long-term notes continued through the summer of 2007. Finally, in September 2007, the Fed became concerned about the inverted yield curve and lowered the Fed funds rate by a full ½ point from 5.25 to 4.75 percent. The Fed then lowered the fed funds rate ten more times until it was zero by December 2008.

But the Fed was not done maiming the American public. In addition to ignoring the warnings of the inverted yield curve, the Fed imposed a monetary policy known as quantitative easing. QE entailed the Fed purchasing Treasury notes to lower interest rates even further than could be accomplished through the lowering of the Fed funds rate. In this case, the Fed purchased $1.7 trillion in U.S. securities creating unnecessary inflation. Inverted yield curves and inflation are the opposite of economic growth and the recipe for a Great Recession. And a Great Recession is exactly what we got lasting from December 2007 through June 2009.

Many economists attribute the subprime mortgage crisis as the cause of the Great Recession, but it was the federal government that created the subprime crisis. (A subprime mortgage is a home loan given to borrowers with a poor credit rating and not enough income to cover monthly principal and interest payments. Subprime loans came mainly in the form of ARM's, Adjustable Rate Mortgages, offering interest-only payments on the first five years of the mortgage. After year five, monthly mortgage payments include current principal, back-principal, plus interest which doubled or tripled the monthly payment.) In the mid-to-late 1990s, the federal government thought it wise to begin enforcement of the Community Reinvestment Act, CRA of 1977. (CRA was created to encourage banking institutions to lend money to moderate and low-income borrowers as a way of reducing discrimination against consumers living in low-income communities.) The government began pressuring mortgage lenders to make loans to people with bad credit scores and no capital available for a down payment. Freddie Mac and Fannie Mae – two federal government chartered financial institutions - were charged with buying high-risk loans from private mortgage lending institutions. Once lenders realized that Freddie and Fannie would buy bad loans, mortgage lenders began handing out over-sized loans like Santa Claus giving out candy canes to children in December. Housing prices skyrocketed in the early 2000s due to rising demand. It wasn't just those with bad credit who were taking advantage of the guaranteed mortgages. Middle class Americans with good credit began trading their average sized homes for much larger and expensive homes dubbed as McMansions. By 2004, home prices were 10 to 20 percent higher than real market value. Combine the subprime mortgage giveaway with the higher cost of real estate, with the Fed's numerous Fed funds rate hikes in 2004, 2005, and 2006, and you have a prescription for disaster. Why? During the height of the subprime mortgage bonanza, new home construction exploded. New housing developments were going up all over the country to meet consumer demands. Money was plentiful and cheap. Then came the Fed funds rate increases beginning in 2004. A raising fed funds rate decreases the quantity of money in circulation making borrowing more expensive as interest rates increase. As money tightened, Americans stopped buying houses. Instead of a shortage, there was now an over-abundance of available homes for sale. Like any other business, when inventory surpasses demand sellers lower prices. And home prices did fall, by as much as 30 percent of true market value. At the same time, subprime mortgage borrowers were being hit with newly adjusted mortgage payments as outlined in the mortgage agreement. Homeowners who could not afford the new payments, and there were seven million of them, lost their homes to foreclosure. And big banks still holding residential mortgage-backed securities were in danger of collapse.

Then it began. On September 15, 2008, Lehman Brothers, the fourth-largest investment bank in the United States filed for bankruptcy. The news saw the DOW drop by some 500 points. The next day, September 16, the Fed agreed to bail out the troubled insurance giant, American International Group (AIG) with an $85 billion line of credit. This was a mistake as AIG was an insurance company and not a bank. The Fed had no regulatory authority over insurance corporations. (AIG sold insurance on just about any financial instrument, but at this time in history it was heavily invested in backing mortgage derivative trades by the big banks. Derivatives are purchased securities gambling on a specific future price of a commodity, bond, stock, currency, mortgages, or even interest rate. If you guess correctly, you make money. If you guess incorrectly, you lose money. Banks purchased insurance from AIG to cover bad guesses. And there were many – billions of dollars' worth of bad mortgage guesses. Unfortunately, AIG never bothered to put money aside to pay potential claims.)

According to a Congressional Oversight Report, [11] the Fed lent AIG $12 billion on September 16, 2008, and another $12 billion on September 17, 2008, to help stabilize operations and stop the bleeding. It did not stop the depletion of assets. As the Fed poured money into the front door of AIG, it left through the back door to big banks to cover their derivative losses. It was like giving a patient a blood transfusion in the arm while he bleeds out through an open wound in the leg. Two months and $182 billion later the Fed closed the line of credit. However, how they did so seems to be another erroneous decision. The Fed created a special program named, "Maiden Lane II." Under ML2, the Fed purchased all residential mortgage-backed securities from AIG. The originators of these securities were big banks who had been selling these securities on the open market for less than 50 cents on the dollar. The Fed purchased the residential mortgage-backed securities at full face value price spending another unnecessary $43.8 billion of taxpayer money.

Perhaps the biggest mistake of Fed interference with AIG's financial difficulties was putting more importance on saving the derivative market over protecting American citizens' savings and checking accounts. But the Fed did not stop at derivative protection with AIG. In September 2008, the Fed designated two investment banks, Morgan Stanley and Goldman Sachs, as bank holding companies.

With this new status, Morgan and Goldman could gain access to emergency federal funds at the Fed discount window – no questions asked. This might have passed as a preemptive move to protect savings and checking accounts had Morgan Stanley not held $9.2 trillion in credit derivatives. Not only was this the largest amount owned by any bank but it was four times greater than Morgan's assets. The Congressional Oversight Panel concluded, *"The rescue of AIG distorted the marketplace by transforming highly risky derivative bets into fully guaranteed payment obligations. The result was that the government backed up the entire derivatives market, as if these trades deserved the same taxpayer backstop as savings deposits and checking accounts."*[12]

Besides AIG there were still big banks, including Citigroup and Bank of America, in trouble. On September 20, 2008, the Fed sent Congress a bank bailout bill. Congress rejected the bill on September 29, 2008, and the stock market plummeted by nearly 800 points. People panicked and stopped spending. With less spending came higher unemployment and lower corporate margins. Diminished corporate earnings depressed stock prices and moved the stock market in a downward direction. And down the stock market went. By March of 2009, the market had dropped to 6,500 and lost more than half of its total value. (In October 2007, the stock market was sitting at 14,100.) Although the Great Recession was declared dead in June 2009, it wasn't until November 2009 when the DOW had recovered and grown by 59 percent to reach the 10,000 plateau. Many economists believe the Fed's manipulation of interest rates was the biggest contributor to the financial crisis of 2008. Part of the reason for this is in addition to a low Federal funds rate; the Fed had been purchasing bonds as a way to keep long-term interest rates down. Of course, these two maneuvers also helped the federal government by keeping debt payments on a $3 trillion liability artificially low. It was the average middle class American saving for retirement, or a rainy day, who suffered most from near zero interest rates. By keeping the interest rates artificially low over for eight years (2008-2016), the Fed made middle class Americans poorer by reducing income generated through savings.

Beginning in December 2008, the Fed lowered the overnight interest rates, or Federal funds rate, to zero and has kept it close to zero for eight years. The Fed considers a healthy Federal funds rate to fall between 2-5 percent, with two percent inflation the ideal target. But low Federal funds rates between 2009 and 2016 did not stimulate the economy as predicted by the Fed as employment and household income remained depressed. As the Fed continued to keep the interest rates low, banks fearful of another recession raised criteria for borrowers making it more difficult for entrepreneurs to get capital to start or grow a business. (Working capital allows small business owners to manufacture more products that create new jobs. Employment drives the economy and creates new wealth.)

Local Banks and the Fed

What about your local bank? What effect do the Federal funds rate and the Fed monetary policy have on them? It makes a significant impact on how local banks approach consumer credit and interests rates. Remember the housing bubble crises of 2008? The federal government charged Fannie Mae and Freddie Mac with buying high-risk loans from private lending institutions. Once Wall Street banks realized that Freddie and Fannie would buy bad loans, mortgage lenders began handing out over-sized loans to middle class citizens who wanted, but could not afford, a larger home. After all, the banker made his money up front from Freddie and Fannie. No waiting thirty years for the borrowers to repay. Instant profit paid in full by Uncle Sam. And the more bad loans private lenders could sell to Freddie and Fannie, the more risk-free money the banks made. If the homeowner defaulted on the loan, Freddie and Fannie—not the lending institution—suffered the loss.

Local bankers loan money to their prime, or best qualified, customers at an interest rate set at three percentage points above the Federal funds rate. A

0.50 federal funds rate will guide bankers to set a 3.50 prime lending rate. Remember, the prime rate is only available to highest creditworthy borrowers, usually large corporations with large profit margins. So what would it cost for an average American to open a line of credit or credit card from the local bank? Currently, if you have a good credit rating (690 – 719), as the average American does (695), a new credit card rate would run about 14.56 percent. That breaks out to prime (3.50 percent) plus a margin, or profit, of 11.06 percent. The Fed caps the first year interest rate at 25 percent, including non-penalty fees. That means the bank can set your credit card rate anywhere between 0.50 percent to as high as 25 percent for year one of use. Do you see a disconnect? Banks can loan money to each other at a rate of 0.50 percent. Or banks can borrow from the Fed at 1.0 percent. But the consumer gets no such discount. Why?

To answer that question we must acknowledge that banks are a business. And like all other businesses, banks strive to earn a profit. Banks earn profits through a variety of ways. There are mortgage loans, auto loans, commercial loans, credit cards, banking fees and service charges, and stock market trading. But banks are making big profits. For example, during the second quarter of 2016, bank profits were recorded at $40.24 billion. So why are interest rates on savings accounts so dismal?

Raising the Federal funds rate two percentage points would raise the prime lending rate by the same amount, and consequently, raise the cost for an average American to borrow money at a rate of at least 16.56 percent, assuming the bank keeps the same margin.

But that is not the biggest disconnect between savers and borrowers. The same rules do not apply to interest rates paid by banks to saving account customers. (There are no federal regulations on interest paid to savers.) The current rate on savings accounts is only slightly higher than one percent. This discrepancy between borrowing and saving interest rates would be understandable if all bank loans were all high-risk loans. They aren't as local banks tend to avoid high-risk loans.

But what is even more perplexing is the Fed pays ever bank a six percent annual tax-free dividend for being part of the Federal Reserve System. Yet the bank doesn't pay six percent interest on your savings account. For banks in existence over 17 years, the Fed dividend is free money. Here is why. Ever member of the Fed is required to buy stock in their regional Federal Reserve Bank. (Every nationally chartered bank must join the Fed. Banks chartered by a specific state are not required to join the Federal Reserve Banking System but are governed by the Fed.) The purchase must equal six percent of the bank's total capital. In reality, the bank only has to purchase three percent as the remaining three percent stays with the local bank on call. When the bank's capital increases or decreases, the bank either pays more to the Federal Reserve Bank or receives a refund for the difference in capital gained or lost. But here is the kicker. After 17 years of membership, the Fed returns the total stock purchase (not adjusted for inflation) to the bank. Dividends received after 17 years then becomes total free money for member banks.

Summary of Federal Reserve System Assault on America

The Federal Reserve System was created to protect the banks', and their customers, liquid assets by providing secured loans to banks should they become undercapitalized. The idea was simple. The Fed was to exist as a rainy day emergency fund for banks that ran into a temporary crisis. But like most government entities the simple becomes complex. Not content to serve as a monetary safety net for the American saver, the Fed has transformed itself into the warden of America's credit allocation. By raising or lowering the Fed funds rate, the Federal Reserve decides who gets financing and who doesn't. It decides who will gain wealth and who will go bankrupt. Fed manipulation of interest rates has a long history of stymieing economic expansion and middle class wealth through the creation of unnecessary and unwanted inflation.

The Fed has misused its powers to:

- Destroy Midwestern farmers during the 1920's
- Protect Wall Street banks while watching local rural banks fail
- Put the country into a 1920-21 recession that reduced national manufacturing goods by $15 billion, created mass unemployment, and devalued land held by ranchers by $20 billion
- Bail out England's banks in 1924, so they could repay WWI loans to Wall Street banks.
- Encourage average Americans, during the mid-1920s to borrow from banks to purchase stocks on margins.
- Stand idly by during 1929 and watch the money supply decline by one-third turning a routine cyclical recession into the Great Depression of 1929 – 1932.
- Allow the Bank of the United States to crash in 1930 wiping out 400,000 depositors and $200 million - defeating the whole purpose of the Fed's creation.
- Raise bank reserve requirements three times in 1936 and 1937, doubling reserve requirements. The resulting consequence was a 13-month recession that led to a 19 percent

unemployment rate and a 32 percent decline in manufacturing.

- Create a steep recession lasting 10 months from August 1957 to April 1958 by slowing economic growth by decreasing the money supply.
- Create an inflationary era lasting from 1965 through 1980 leading to two recessions during the 1970s. The first, in 1970, lasted for 11 months. The second and more damaging recession lasted from November 1973 to March 1975. Fed funds rates were at 13 percent, inflation 12 percent, unemployment was at nine percent, and the price of gasoline quadrupled creating shortages at the pumps.
- Raise the Fed funds rate in March 1980 from 10.25 percent to 20 percent and keep it there until May 1981. This created the worst recession since 1929 lasting from July 1981 until November 1982. Unemployment hit 11 percent with manufacturing job losses at 75 percent of all lost jobs.
- Effectively shut down the Savings and Loans industry by preventing S&Ls from offering depositors competitive interest rates. The Fed was responsible for the closing of nearly 1,800 S&Ls worth about $400 billion in assets.
- Keep the inflation rate at three percent, one full percentage point higher than

recommended by economists for the better part of the 1990s.

- Triggered a financial crises in 2007 which brought America to its knees.
- Raised the Fed fund rate in 2004 creating an inverted yield curve on short-term and long-term Treasury notes. Knowing full well that an inverted yield curve is a precursor to a recession, the Fed continued to throw caution to the wind by raising the Fed funds rate even higher. The inverted yield curve continued to grow larger by each passing month. Finally, in September 2007, the Fed decided to lower the Fed funds rate by a full ½ point from 5.25 to 4.75 percent. This was too little too late. And the Great Recession of 2007-2009 was upon us courtesy of the Fed.

It is written that history serves as a lesson to prevent future miscues. If that's the case, the Fed and its many governors have not studied their history very well. Both the Great Depression of 1929-1932 and the Great Recession of 2007-2009 took a heavy toll on middle class America. Jobs, savings, homes, and lives were needlessly lost due to an inept and sometimes malfeasant Fed. The very structure that was created to protect middle class savings choose to abdicate its responsibility in favor of sheltering the assets of the wealthy.

Both the Great Depression and Great Recession were created by asset bubbles caused by a flood of easy credit. In the 1920s the bubble was stocks and securities purchased by average Americans on margins with borrowed money. In the late 1990s and early 2000s, it was cheap credit to purchase houses. The Fed created these bubbles by manipulating interest rates from low to high and high to low snuffing out economic growth when it was most needed. The bubbles were burst because the Fed's actions devalued, or watered down, the asset bubbles held by consumers leaving them underwater with no escape route.

In both the Great Depression and Great Recession, the Fed allowed banks to use a technique known as securitization. Essentially this process allows banks to originate and repackage various and highly speculative loans. The loans are then sold as securities on the open market through reputable dealers. In the 1920s securitization consisted of loans made to average Americans to purchase stocks. In the late 1990s and early 2000s, it was high-risk mortgage loans.

Another comparison between the two waves of panic to consider is much of the Fed's failed policies and actions taken in the 1920s were directed by the New York Federal Reserve Bank, which was controlled by powerful Wall Street bankers. Today, the New York Federal Reserve Bank is yet considered the king of all Federal Reserve banks and is still ruled by a former Wall Street banker. This should be no surprise as the Fed, since inception in 1913, states that the president of a Federal Reserve Bank shall be the chief executive officer of a Bank and selected by the board of directors of that Bank.

One final comparison of the Fed's failure between the panics of 1929 and 2008. In both cases, the Fed choose to rescue the speculative market over the protection of middle class assets and savings. This sent a message that high-risk financial behaviors on the part of the financial community are acceptable and will be protected over the rights of average American citizens. Securitization will continue as a Wall Street practice as long as they are rewarded for bad behavior.

With its unlimited power to create money out of thin air, the Fed has created financial panics, burst economic bubbles, and involved the United States in a world war. The Fed has put average Americans into the proverbial poor house while destroying trillions of dollars of citizens' wealth. The Fed has continually interfered with capitalism and free markets while controlling the distribution of wealth. It's time to fix the Fed.

How Do We Get Control?

To be sure, the Federal Reserve System has demonstrated over its 100-year history that it simply does not work. It has not been the stabilizing force of the economy by which it was created to do. It has accomplished just the opposite. The Fed has destroyed, rather than protect the wealth of the average American citizen. We have no monetary integrity, and we desperately need it. So how do we get it?

Some Federal Reserve would-be reformers and economists believe the Fed should be moved into the Treasury Department where it would be subject to congressional oversight. The problem with this idea is it would give Congress free rein to second-guess monetary policy. Just what America needs. More opportunities for meddling know-nothing bureaucrats to conspire with banking elites to keep middle-class Americans struggling to make ends meet. And undoubtedly, Congress under the guise of checks and balances would pass regulations to protect the people from Fed policies that would have just the opposite effect. No, moving the Fed under the Treasury or any other government agency is not the answer.

Other Fed reformers want to shorten the term limits of the Fed chairpersons and require selection by the president and approval by Congress. Shorter terms would not change the structure of the Fed or how it operates. Each chairperson reports to a board of directors comprised of powerful bankers and thus the regional chair has limited powers. Selection by the president only ensures a political appointment will be made and nothing more. It would have no positive effect on the operation of the Fed since that power is in the hands of the chair of the Federal Reserve Bank System, who is appointed by the president.

Yet another reform proposal would compel the Fed to use a mathematical formula to prescribe its monetary policy decisions. The Taylor rule, as it is known, is a forecasting model used to determine what interest rates should be as shifts in the economy occur. The end result of this proposal is math rather than a human would be in charge of manipulating interest rates. Enough of will not work. Let's look at a couple of ideas that might work.

Proposal 1: Free Market

To reform the Fed, one basic question needs to be answered. Should the Fed be allowed to manipulate interest rates in the first place? We have seen and lived through the horrendous results of the Fed massaging the economy through interest rate hikes and dips and know that rate manipulation hurts rather than helps. That is because, essentially, interest rate manipulation is nothing more than a price control. Government price controls define the market price and force all transactions to take place at that price instead of an equilibrium price set through supply and demand. Money supply and demand constantly shift in response to tastes, innovations, and life circumstances, but government prices change only after a lengthy political process meaning the government price will never be an equilibrium price. This means that the government price will be either too high or too low. We saw this in the 1920s, 30s, 50s, 70s, 80s, and again in the 2000s. Government price controls, like manipulation of interest rates, don't work.

Currently, the Fed sets the price lenders to pay borrowers for the use of money. Shouldn't borrowers and lenders settle on a price the same way as a buyer and seller negotiate a price on a house, car, or television set? Free competition for borrowers and lenders would determine market prices through the process of supply and demand. Customer preferences for a money product would determine how much they will buy at any given price. Banks, in turn, would be free to decide how much they are willing to supply at different prices. A free market competitive process will create an equilibrium market price where banks and customers transact freely at a price that exactly equals supply and demand.

Proposal 2: Public Company

a.) Treat the Federal Reserve Banking System like a publicly traded company indexed to a stock exchange. The Fed currently issues stocks guaranteed to yield six percent dividends to member banks only. Require the Fed to hold an initial public offering (IPO) allowing all citizens the opportunity to purchase shares and generate revenue from the Fed. Revenue generated by the Fed through the sale of shares would be used to purchase long and short-term Treasury notes providing the liquidity needed should a bank failure occur as well as dividend revenue for shareholders. (For once the Fed would actually use real money to purchase the notes which would actually help fund the government while keeping inflation under control.)

b.) With stock ownership comes voting rights to determine the management team and overall direction of the Fed. Selection of chairpersons and board of governors would switch from the president and career politicians to stockholders.

c.) The Federal Reserve System was created to be the lender of the last resource to banks experiencing a run on withdrawals. The intent was to protect the savings of American citizens. Let's keep that concept intact and eliminate the deadly game of interest manipulation. The Fed should have one task and only one task, provide liquidity to banks if they get in financial trouble.

Proposal 3: True Insurance

Every bank in America would pay an annual insurance premium based on previous year's total assets – similar to how life insurance premiums are based on age and amount of desired coverage.

Like Proposal 2, the Fed would:

- a.) Be required to purchase both short and long-term Treasury notes to cover potential liquidity issues.
- b.) No longer be permitted to manipulate bank interest rates.

Unlike Proposal 2, no dividends would be paid to banks. The annual payment paid to the Fed is simply an insurance premium.

I think the best solution would be a combination of proposal 1 and 2, or proposal 1 and 3. Our country is based on the free market system so it makes sense to include the banking business within the competitive marketplace.

Crazy Mark Proposal: QE for citizens

Instead of a using quantitative easing, QE, to purchase Treasury notes to lower interest rates, why not just increase the money supply of the average American? Spending is the engine that drives the economy, and there are no better spenders than the middle class. Banks and rich people do not spend; they purchase securities.

Just imagine how quickly the economy could have recovered in 2009 if the Fed had flooded middle class Americans rather than financial institutions with $1.7 trillion. If each of America's middle class adults were given an equal portion of the Fed's QE, each middle class adult would have received $14,000. Most of that money would have, in turn, been returned to the economy through the purchasing of products and services. That is what makes an economy thrive. Instead, the Fed's use of QE moved more middle class Americans into the lower class while making the wealthy richer. So how about it Fed? If you want the economy to work, issue a $1.7 trillion QE for American adults.

CHAPTER 2. Wall Street Banks Control Big Business and Washington

"I believe that banking institutions are more dangerous to our liberties than standing armies. If the American people ever allow private banks to control the issue of their currency, first by inflation, then by deflation, the banks and corporations that will grow up around the banks will deprive the people of all property until their children wake-up homeless on the continent their fathers conquered."
– Thomas Jefferson 1802

I can think of no better way to begin this chapter than a reprint of a speech given on June 24, 2008, by the late comedian George Carlin titled, "The Real Owners of America."

"The real owners are the big wealthy business interests that control things and make all the important decisions. Forget the politicians, they're an irrelevancy. The politicians are put there to give you the idea that you have freedom of choice. You don't. You have no choice. You have owners. They own you. They own everything. They own all the important land. They own and control the corporations. They've long since bought and paid

for the Senate, the Congress, the statehouses, the city halls. They've got the judges in their back pockets. And they own all the big media companies, so that they control just about all of the news and information you hear. They've got you by the balls. They spend billions of dollars every year lobbying - lobbying to get what they want. Well, we know what they want; they want more for themselves and less for everybody else."

Perhaps Carlin was right. Let's explore Wall Street within the context of Mr. Carlin's argument.

Wall Street banks are commonly referred to as investment banks as they sell a wide variety of financial products such as derivatives, equities, currency, and commodities to name a few. They are large multinational corporations conducting business throughout the globe. They are different from your small local bank that provides limited financial services such as savings, checking, and money market accounts to a small regional geographic area. Wall Street banks usually hold assets in the trillions whereas local banks may hold less than a billion. In fact, America's top four Wall Street banks held assets totaling about $7.1 trillion in 2016. The other 8,091 banks covered by the FDIC had assets worth about $5.9 trillion. Holdings for the average American, however, are quite different. In 2016, it was estimated that the average American had just under $4,500 in their checking account. Approximately 62 percent of Americans had less than $1,000 in their savings account with another 21 percent with no savings account at all.

So it seems that Jefferson's fear of big, powerful banks might be more real than ever. And for a good reason. In addition to the trillions of dollars in assets, Wall Street controls corporate manufacturing decisions, executive hiring and firings, corporate profit margins, and influences who is elected to Congress and the office of President. In other words, Wall Street controls the economy, the government, the stock market, and America's future. The creation of the Federal Reserve Bank failed to eliminate Wall Street's power over America's financial system. It did the opposite; it gave them immense power. Let's take a look.

For example, let's examine how Wall Street influence hurt one American company. The *Harvard Business Review* cites Boeing Corporation as a case study on Wall Street's negative influence.[13] In the aerospace manufacturing industry Boeing has a history of innovation and superior quality. Its clients include major airlines, NASA, and the Department of Defense. But sometime in the late 1990s, Boeing's upper management began to focus on Wall Street corporate financial expectations. One metric in particular that worried Boeing was RONA or return on net assets. (RONA is a ratio of income to assets.) RONA is one of the main metrics used by Wall Street to judge companies and their management. An unfavorable company analysis from Wall Street usually lowers the value of corporate stock and the affordable of capital available for operations or growth opportunities. Despite objections of senior engineers, Boeing began outsourcing major components for its new aircraft, the 787, to maximize RONA. (Outsourcing removes the outsourced components from a company's balance sheet making the RONA ratio more favorable. But outsourcing also hinders a company's ability to manage quality control and R&D, to negotiate lower supplier prices through volume purchasing, and to meet government regulations on material sourcing, human rights, and child labor.) Outsourcing the 787 components created a complicated supply chain and difficulty with maintaining a high standard of quality control. Outsourced components failed to meet Boring standards at an alarming rate. Boeing suffered massive cost and time overruns with launching the 787. Boeing had expected to spend $5 billion to develop the 787. Fixing all of the mistakes made by outsourced components cost Boeing another $18 billion. When all was said and done, and production of the 787 began, Boeing lost about $25 million on each plane.

Pleasing Wall Street had a high price tag. And in the end, after Boeing's 787 failed delivery, Wall Street analysts downgraded Boeing's stock in April 2016 to underperform. Its stock price fell 8.2 percent. (An underperforming rating leads to declining stock prices which stifles consumer desire for the brand, frightens suppliers, and produces a loss in sales. All of which reduces the cash flow needed to support healthy operations and a positive bottom line.) At the conclusion of 2016, Boeing airplane sales fell short of its targeted goal by 80 planes. Boeing plane orders for 2016 were at their lowest since 2010 while its book to bill ratio of new sales to deliveries fell to its lowest level since 2004. Boeing also cut its workforce by 4,500. Many financial analysts believe Boeing will never recover loses or make a profit on the 787.

While Boeing management alone must assume all responsibility for the failures associated with the development and production of the 787, Wall Street certainly influenced Boeing decision-making. But Boeing is not alone. Wall Street punishes corporate executives who do not heed their advice. Wall Street's influence on business decisions is domineering. So much so that *"A recent survey of chief financial officers showed that 78% would 'give up economic value' and 55% would cancel a project with a positive net present value — that is, willingly harm their companies — to meet Wall Street's targets and fulfill its desire for 'smooth' earnings."* [14] The CEO of

Sara Lee, a company that produces baked goods, sausages, leather handbags, and athletic clothes put it this way. *"Wall Street can wipe you out. They are the rule-setters. They do have their fads, but to a large extent there is an evolution in how they judge companies, and they have decided to give premiums to companies that harbor the most profits for the least assets."*[15]

Wall Street also calls the shots over business mergers and acquisitions. Now you might be tempted into thinking that when one company buys or merges with another, it is to gain a competitive advantage of some sort, perhaps product innovation or advanced technology. That might happen occasionally, but for the most part, companies merge to please Wall Street in hopes of making a quick buck. There can be no other reason as the failure rate for mergers and acquisitions ranges from an astonishing 70 to 90 percent.[16] In addition to the thousands of jobs lost as a result of mergers and acquisitions, the business puts its long-term survival in jeopardy for fear that Wall Street will put them out of business in the short-term through underperforming ratings. McKinsey and Company predict that sometime before 2025, seven out of 10 of the largest companies will come from emerging countries whose businesses have long-term profit mindsets and not be located within the United States. It further believes these top businesses will be family-owned and not indexed on the stock market; meaning no Wall Street connections or influences.

Yes, big business has clearly been hijacked by Wall Street. Case in point, Dell Computer Company. Michael Dell founded Dell Computers in his college dorm room in 1984. In 1988, Dell took his company public through an IPO, Initial Public Offering, and raised $30 million for operations and expansion. By 1992, Dell Computers were on the Fortune 500 list of biggest companies. By 2001, Dell Computers were the number one selling computer system in the world. In 2004 Michael Dell resigned as CEO of Dell with the intention of focusing on his philanthropic foundation. Soon after, in 2006, Dell underperformed to Wall Street expectations and began losing market share to HP. Concerned about the company he founded, Michael Dell came out of retirement and became CEO in 2007. Wall Street didn't take kindly to Dell's return to power. They viewed him as a one trick pony who had nothing new to add to Dell Computers. Wall Street analysts continued to push Dell's share price in a downward direction. Even after a 2012 fiscal year that saw Dell earn $62 billion in revenue with a profit of just over $3 billion, Wall Street kept piling on unfavorable reports. They choose to focus only on declining PC sales and ignored Dell's transformation into a $21 billion IT services company that complemented the PC small business line.

By 2013, Michael Dell had enough of outside investor influences and Wall Street bullying. He raised $25 billion in private funds to purchase all outstanding shares of Dell stock taking the company back into private hands and away from Wall Street. Free from Wall Street analysts and activist investors who wanted short-term revenue at the expense of long-term stability, Dell was able to follow his aspirations of becoming a one-stop technology and services vendor for small to mid-sized companies. As of January 2016, Dell employed nearly 102,000 workers and posted annual revenue of $55 billion.

Then there is PetSmart, a retailer specializing in pet supplies founded in 1986. By 1992, PetSmart operated 50 retail stores. To raise capital for further expansion, PetSmart offered an IPO in 1993. A year after going public, PetSmart operated 100 stores. By 2007, 1,000 stores existed. But all was not what it could be at PetSmart. Wall Street pressured PetSmart's management to return high quarterly cash returns to stockholders over long-term growth goals. To meet Wall Street expectations, PetSmart skimped on advertising and marketing costs. A smaller than average advertising budget yielded smaller annual growth.

Although a bigger advertising budget would have helped PetSmart's long-term growth strategy, the real problem was the funneling of ROIC, Return on

Invested Capital, into meeting Wall Street's demand for short-term cash. PetSmart had grown its ROIC by a healthy 36 percent between 2008 and 2014, but it was spending all its free cash flow on stock dividend payments and buybacks rather than investing in new opportunities. PetSmart management recognized that a short-term bump in stock price destroys long-term investment opportunities leaving the company ripe for future bankruptcy. To their credit, PetSmart's board and senior management negotiated an $8.7 billion private buyout taking PetSmart off the publicly traded stock market.

Dell and PetSmart are not the only companies to go private and escape Wall Street's death grip. According to the 2016 Wilshire 5000 Total Market Index, just 3,818 companies are traded publicly. In 1998, 7,562 companies had publicly listed stocks.

Wall Street banks are like army ants. When they find a company they feel is underperforming, or not returning enough short-term revenue to stockholders, they attack en masse. They are swarm raiders. Wall Street rips apart and destroys its prey piece-by-piece leaving nothing but picked clean bones and unemployed workers. Then they move on to the next target. This migration of death kills corporate innovation, stagnates middle class wages, and prolongs unemployment. Wall Street cares little for the individuals who rely on indexed stock companies for a weekly paycheck and quality products. They are concerned only with enriching the pockets of wealthy shareholders with quick cash at the expense of the business and economy.

Wall Street Owns Washington

In 1914, Jack Morgan, Jr sent this message to President Woodrow Wilson. *"The war should be a tremendous opportunity for America."*[17] Morgan was, of course, referring to the beginning of World War I. Wilson wanted to stay neutral believing the United States could serve as the peace-keeper. Morgan wanted to loan money to France to help in the war effort. Not because he had any political interest in seeing France win buy rather, Morgan was aware that his grandfather, a London banker, had lent France $50 million during the Franco-Prussian war of 1870. The elder Morgan made a tidy profit. Jack Morgan saw another opportunity to make money on a French war. In September 1914, Morgan and his J.P. Morgan Bank provided France with a $100 million line of credit. Then in August of 1915, Morgan pulled together a few other Wall Street bankers and lent the British and French governments $500 million for their war efforts. Loans this large, $100 million and $500 million, do not go unnoticed. The U.S. press knew and reported on the loans. It is a good bet that the Central Powers (Germany, the Austro-Hungarian Empire, the Ottoman Empire, and

Bulgaria) also knew of the loan to the Triple Entente (France, Britain, and Russia). So much for neutrality. Especially when Wilson gave Morgan his blessing and approved the loans.

The Woodrow Wilson President and Jack Morgan Wall Street banker relationship was not an exception in Washington politics. Wall Street bankers have influenced presidents and infiltrated high-level federal government cabinet positions ever since.

- Warren Harding appointed Andrew Mellon, owner of the Union Trust Company and Union Savings Bank of Pittsburgh, Secretary of Treasury. He held that position through the Coolidge and Hoover administrations.
- FDR's elections were financed with major contributions from Sidney Weinberg, who was president of Goldman Sachs from 1930-1969. Weinberg also had close ties to Truman, Eisenhower, JFK, LBJ, and Nixon.
- Truman's Secretary of Treasury, John Snyder, was a close friend of the founder of the Bank of America.
- Eisenhower selected Thomas Gates, Chairman and CEO of Morgan Guaranty Trust Bank, as Secretary of Defense.
- David Rockefeller, Chairman of Chase Bank, served as an advisor to JFK, LBJ, Nixon, and Ford.

- LBJ selected Henry Fowler, a partner at Goldman Sachs as his Secretary of Treasury.
- Ronald Reagan choose Donald Regan, Chairman of Merrill Lynch, as Secretary of Treasury.
- John Reed, Chairman of Citicorp, advised George H.W. Bush and Bill Clinton.
- Bill Clinton selected Robert Rubin, Cochairman of Goldman Sachs as Secretary of Treasury.
- Barack Obama selected Timothy Geithner, president of the New York Federal Reserve as Secretary of Treasury.
- Donald Trump has selected Steven Mnuchin, former Goldman Sachs partner and head of Dune Capital Management, as his Secretary of Treasury.

Washington and Wall Street are joined at the hip. But who controls who? Relationships between the two sometimes seem to be so incestuous that it is hard to determine who works for the government from who works for Wall Street. But nevertheless, Presidents of the United States wield tremendous power and have fended off Wall Street pressures when they wanted to. This may not be the case in the 21st century going forward. *"The Bush and Obama presidencies represented a climax in the development of relationships and codependent actions that began with Teddy Roosevelt. But whereas Roosevelt, Wilson, FDR, Eisenhower, and Johnson had nursed synergies that enabled useful public-oriented legislation. Bush and Obama had become followers and reactors to bankers' whims. By the 2000s, bankers no longer debated economic policy in thoughtful correspondences with presidents or Treasury secretaries, as they once had."*[18]

In addition to holding high cabinet positions and presidential advisor roles, Wall Street bankers also control Washington politics through campaign contributions. Wall Street wants politicians who will support banker interests. Make no mistake that bankers' concerns are not about sharing the wealth or creating policies to help the poor and middle class. We often hear about the greed of the top 1.0 percent, but most of them are not that influential. It is the top 0.1 percent who control the banks and government policy. It is the top 0.1 percent who hold as much wealth as the bottom 90 percent. They contribute hundreds of millions to political campaigns by creating super PACs (political action committees), which have no limits on contribution amounts. Super PACs raised nearly $776 million in the 2016 Presidential election. Another $636 million was spent on the Senate while 2016 House of Representatives saw $313 million spent on their races.[19] The top 100 individual donors contributed from $1.3 million all the way up to $86 million.

Lobbying is another tool used by Wall Street to control Washington politicians. According to OpenSecrets.org, the finance and insurance industries spent over $7 billion on lobbying between 1998 and 2016.[20] But it doesn't end there.

In 1958, Hollywood produced a movie called The Blob. The film shows a small alien creature with no definition crashing to Earth. It looked like a piece of Jell-O. The storyline depicts this creature engulfing people and growing larger and larger and seemingly unstoppable. Well Washington D.C. has its own version of The Blob.

"The Blob refers to the government entities that regulate the finance industry – like the Banking Committee, Treasury Department, and SEC – and the army of Wall Street representatives and lobbyists that continuously surrounds and permeates them. The Blob moves together. Its members are in constant contact by e-mail and phone. They dine, drink, and take vacations together. Not surprisingly, they frequently intermarry. Indeed a good way to maximize your family income in DC is to specialize in financial issues and marry someone in The Blob. Ideally, you and your spouse take turns: One of you works for a bank, insurance company, or lobbying firm while the other works for a government entity that regulates, or enacts legislation for, the financial

industry. Every few years, you reverse roles. What you and your spouse do all the time is share information. After all, no lobbying restrictions yet promulgated can prevent pillow talk between Blob spouses. Actually, marrying The Blob isn't even necessary. A Blob member can simply take his or her non-Blob spouse to Blob parties – convivial gatherings of lobbyists and Wall Street emissaries, SEC and Treasury Department officials – to help gather and disseminate intelligence, It's a weekly, and sometimes nightly, occurrence in Washington."[21]

The Blob is so effective that bank lobbyists actually help write legislation concerning financial regulations. An article in "Investment Banking" reports the following story. *"One bill that sailed through the House Financial Services Committee this month — over the objections of the Treasury Department — was essentially Citigroup's, according to e-mails reviewed by The New York Times. The bill would exempt broad swathes of trades from new regulation. In a sign of Wall Street's resurgent influence in Washington, Citigroup's recommendations were reflected in more than 70 lines of the House committee's 85-line bill. Two crucial paragraphs, prepared by Citigroup in conjunction with other Wall Street banks, were copied nearly word for word."*[22]

Just like Wall Street stock analysis controls big business, Wall Street money controls Washington politicians. Wall Street finances campaigns of candidates who are friendly toward Wall Street interests and funds smear campaigns of perceived enemies of the banks. Once elected, politicians are pressured to hire Wall Street executives in influential positions. Wall Street bribes the White House and Congress not with money, but with the threat of future attacks against current banking regulations. One such example occurred in December 2014. President Obama fought Democratic lawmakers on Capitol Hill over a single line in legislation intended to keep the Federal government funded for the next several months. That one line in 1,600 pages of political gibberish would allow banks to make risky investments using taxpayer money. The White House favored the bill as was because *"it averted other amendments that would have undercut Dodd-Frank."*[23] The problem with this thinking was risky investments of taxpayer money is exactly what the Dodd-Frank Law protects. Passing this legislation would undo the main provision of Dodd-Frank.

This example goes to show Wall Street control over legislation at a very basic benign manner. Someone in Congress had to insert the line into the legislation. The bill would have passed through several committees before it was brought up for discussion on Capitol Hill. The line could have been struck out by any number of multiple players on multiple occasions. The fact that this one line remained in the legislation after being reviewed multiple times by lawmakers demonstrates the both the fear and loyalty Congress has for Wall Street power.

George Carlin was right. Wall Street owns Washington.

Summary

Wall Street's corporate evaluations and short-term metrics have cost hundreds of thousands of middle class jobs, destroyed businesses, hindered innovation, and kept wages stagnant. Because of Wall Street companies are afraid to reinvest profits in research, job creation and increased employee wages. Instead, they use their cash to buyback stocks or sit on it in banks accounts just to appease Wall Street analytics. These actions hurt the economy, and they hurt the average American by keeping money out of circulation. Spending is the engine of any economy.

But Wall Street has not just been content to ruin businesses, pensions, and the economy through bad banking practices. They have forged a partnership with the Washington elite giving Wall Street almost unlimited powers and opportunities to destroy the American dream. Washington and banker jobs are so interwoven you need a scorecard to determine who's on the field on any given day. The players change uniforms more often than the Cleveland Browns change quarterbacks. When government and bankers operate as one, the middle class loses. And they have.

How Do We Get Control

We are going to need a lot of help to stop the influence of Wall Street because, as we have seen, Wall Street and Washington act as one entity. And the only way we can fix this is through new laws; laws that are made by Washington politicians who serve as puppets of Wall Street. Nevertheless, I make the following proposals with the hope that some in Washington still care about our country.

Proposal 1: Bank Size

Limit the size of banks. The largest banks grew larger and faster after Great Recession of 2008-09. In 1995 the assets of the six largest banks were equivalent to 17 percent of the United States' GDP. In 2006 that number had grown to 55 percent. By 2013 it was 58 percent.

The Office of the Comptroller of the Currency released a report in March 2016 which showed Citigroup alone with total assets of $1.8 trillion and another $55.6 trillion in derivatives. (It held $41 trillion in 2008 when it was bailed out by the government. The bailout provided Citigroup with $350 billion from TARP and another $2 trillion from the Fed.) Of the $55.6 trillion, $52.9 trillion was FDIC insured. In other words, the U.S. government was backing Citigroup's risky investments. And with the next top four banks holding an additional $175.4 trillion in derivatives, the U.S. government would be hard-pressed to cover these losses in the event of another bubble. (Remember, a derivative is a high-risk security – anything that can be traded such as company stock, mortgages, or currency - with an assigned value that is derived from one or more assets. Essentially, it is a bet on a bet. Banks treat derivatives as a form of a deposit or capital. Loans, which produce real income for the bank, are based on the amount of capital on the books. Derivatives artificially increase capital allowing banks to lend more money.)

Big banks engage in risky investments to grow bigger. How big do they need to be? Let's limit their growth to ensure financial and economic stability. Tie growth to annual GDP. A simple metric is bank assets to GDP. This metric measures bank capital to assets of bank capital and reserves to total assets bank debt to GDP ratio. Currently, Citigroup Bank debt equals 10 percent of total GDP. That's too high. For starters, cap the ratio at four percent of GDP. This measure would affect only the largest six or seven banks out a total of 5,083 banks in the United States. Keeping banks small enough to fail without government bailout might just be enough to keep bankers in check when it comes to risky investment. **Combine proposal** 1 with **proposal** 2 for maximum safety.

Proposal 2: Fix Dodd-Frank Wall Street Reform Consumer Protection Act. Restore Section 716

When Dodd-Frank was first passed into law there existed Section 716 commonly known as the Push-Out Rule. This part of the law required banks to eliminate or push-out derivatives to their uninsured affiliates releasing the taxpayer from any financial liability should the bank crash. This rule was to take effect in July 2015. It did not. In 2014, Citigroup lobbyists maneuvered, at the last minute, bank favorable language into a federal omnibus spending bill that was passed just three hours prior to a threatened shutdown of the government due to lack of funding. The inserted banking language repealed Section 716. President Obama was aware of the banking language yet chose to sign the spending bill into law rather than fight the banking industry.

Proposal 3: Term Limits

Currently, the president of the United States is limited to two four-year terms, no more. Senators, on the other hand, can be reelected every six years for as many times as they wish to rub. Likewise, House representatives hold two-year terms and can seek re-election as often as they like. And therein lies the problem, the President is limited to eight years while the Congress can hold office for a lifetime. This is not what our founding fathers envisioned when they created the Republic. Washington, Jefferson, Adams, and others believed offices should be turned over frequently to bring in new ideas and perspectives and to guarantee that the average citizen had a chance to be heard. Our founding fathers knew that career politicians could be bought and sold for a price. They were right. Washington politicians are beholding to banks. Bankers make politicians wealthy. They fund the election campaigns, and they hire them into multimillion dollar salaried positions after they leave office. But there is a fix for this.

Let's limit congressional terms as follows:

- President: keep as is – two four-year terms
- Senate: two six year terms
- House: three four-year terms

By limiting congressional terms, we can reduce opportunities for long-term arrangements between the banking industry and politicians. Once a legislator is elected to the last term, that politician no longer needs to raise campaign funds and cater to bankers' wishes. And if the last term legislator has a soul they may just work for the people or want to leave a legacy of being a champion for the people. It could happen.

Term limits for nonelected senior administration officials are also necessary. Often career politicians hold multiple offices for multiple administrations. Allowing senior level officials with banking ties to stay in Washington for unlimited terms helps the banking industry to maintain its grip on politicians. I propose that all senior and cabinet positions be restricted to the same term limits as the President – two four-year terms or a total of eight years lifetime.

Proposal 4: Non-Compete Clause

Pass legislation that requires bankers to be five years removed from the banking industry prior to a political appointment or financial industry lobbying group. Likewise, require House and Senate representatives to be five years removed from Congress prior to accepting a financial industry position or lobbying position.

Proposal 5: Public Banks

Congress all but killed the Savings and Loan industry, the closest thing to a public bank, in the late 80s and early 90s. Publicly owned, or state government banks, have a place in America. Currently, there is one public bank in the United States, the Bank of North Dakota. Established in 1919 to fight off Wall Street pilfering of Midwestern farms, BND has assists of $ 7.4 billion with reported profits of $130 million in 2015. BND does not engage in risky loans, in dicey derivatives, and does not pay million dollar bonuses to executives.

The North Dakota public bank has complete transparency and accountability - including routine audits by several agencies. It does not pay executives exorbitant salaries and bonuses. It does not reward bankers for churning out risky loans. And it does not engage in investing in risky derivatives. It has lower costs because no advertising is necessary; instead, the government guarantees the bank easy access to liquidity.

A public bank operates the same way as a private bank, except all profits made go to the public, or state government, and not Wall Street. All the revenues earned or collected by the state go into the state's public bank, which then leverages those deposits into credit. The government actually makes money from enterprise activities and returns profits back to the people. Imagine how much money states (the public) would save just on bank fees and interest payments made by the public bank to the state.

According to *Global Finance,*[24] the seven safest banks in the world are publicly owned. No American commercial bank is in the top 40. Let's make it easier to establish public banks giving citizens more banking choices.

Proposal 6: Require SEC hardship approval of company stock buyback.

The U.S. Securities and Exchange Commission (SEC) was designed to be the regulatory watchdog needed to stop stock manipulation and fraud. Yet legal manipulation of stocks through the process known as buybacks has occurred at an alarming rate during the 21st century. Except in rare cases where a stock buyback is needed to keep a company afloat, this process should be illegal. Buybacks decrease the number of company shares held by the public and give an immediate increase in earnings per share of the remaining shareholders. This is a problem because of very rich men and women, known as corporate raiders, buy their way on a company's board of directors through the purchase of seven to 10 percent of the corporate stock. Once on the board, the raider strong-arms the board into buybacks. This results in a tidy profit for the raider as he quickly sells his shares at the newly established premium price. Stock buybacks do not help the economy; they hurt it. Buybacks use profits that could be used to help the company pay better wages, hire more employees, innovate, expand markets, or improve operations.

Proposal 7: Require all large businesses to submit a five-year growth plan to SEC.

Along with the annual incentive plan that companies file with SEC, require a corporate sustainable long-term business growth plan. Components of the plan should include:

- Data driven information
- Desired innovation supporting core business development
- Integrated involvement from board, employees, and customers
- Targeted annual revenue growth
- Strategy for achieving objectives in plan
- Capital to be invested during plan

The general idea here is to give corporations a weapon, supported by the SEC, to beat back negative Wall Street analytics.

CHAPTER 3. Education

"But I'll tell you what they (Wall Street elite) don't want. They don't want a population of citizens capable of critical thinking. They don't want well-informed, well-educated people capable of critical thinking. They're not interested in that. That doesn't help them. That's against their interests. They don't want people who are smart enough to sit around the kitchen table and figure out how badly they're getting f****d by a system that threw them overboard 30 f*****g years ago." - George Carlin

Somewhat of a provocative statement from a comedian. Yet somehow Carlin's remarks strike a chord. Education is thought to be the great equalizer, the one thing necessary for social equality, a strong middle class, and an essential component for the life, liberty, and pursuit of happiness as a free people. Yet too many Americans seem to be missing out on the opportunity to receive a true education, partly because the opportunity is not there. I am not just referring to public education in low-income neighborhoods. Rather I include the college educated at all levels. And it's not their fault. The wealthy elite controls all levels of the education system and recognizes that an educated populace is the singularly most potent threat to their power and affluence. Let's examine some of the popular recurring themes to see if we can make some sense out of the messages.

College for Everyone

Is college for all really a good idea? Politicians and the media tell us it is. But are they thinking about what is best for you and the future of America? Let's find out.

The number one argument for college for all is that a four-year degree is the only door into the middle class. That is just plain nonsense. According to a CNBC report, *"51 percent of graduates from the classes of 2014 and 2015 said they are working in jobs that do not require their college degree. And 39 percent of graduates from the classes of 2014 and 2015 are making $25,000 or less."*[25] Over half of all college graduates can't find work in their field of study while almost 40 percent earn the equivalent of $12 per hour or less. Imagine what the job market might look like if every adult American held a college degree? It's very likely that only about 25 percent or less of graduates would find work in their field. Wages would go down as there would be no shortage of qualified individuals waiting to fill vacant positions. Do these numbers seem like keys to the middle class?

In 2015, the IBM Institute for Business Value conducted a survey of more than 900 university professors and leaders of major corporations as well as interviews with 25 leading academic subject matter experts.[26] They found:

- 49 percent of industry and academic leaders believed higher education met student needs.
- 41 percent believed it met industry's needs.
- 43 percent across industry and academia believed higher education prepared students with necessary workforce skills.
- 58 percent of academic leaders believed their top priority was to maintain tight uniformity across course requirements.
- 55 percent of academic leaders believed their top priority was to maximize seats filled at the university.
- 51 percent of academic leaders believed their priority was to seek funding from external business and government institutions.
- 66 percent of academic leaders said they did not want to collaborate with external business to define curricula.
- 76 percent of academic leaders said universities are not in the business of launching careers.

Education

A survey conducted by Harris Interactive in August 2013, interviewed 2,001 18-24-year-olds enrolled in college and 1,000 hiring managers.[27] This survey found:

- 39 percent of hiring managers said the recent college graduates they have interviewed were prepared for a job in their field of study.
- 51 percent of hiring managers said recent graduates could not write or communicate ideas clearly.
- 70 percent of hiring managers said graduates could not create a budget or financial goal

Still think college for all is a good idea? Universities are currently failing a majority of their graduates. Why would we want to grow the number of young people with college debt and a degree that does not provide graduates with the skills they need to move into the workforce?

During the 2016 presidential campaign, Hillary Clinton, nominee for the Democratic Party, did more than back the idea of college for all Americans. She went further and espoused free tuition at all public colleges and universities throughout the country for any student of a family earning less than $125,000 per year. (Students enrolled at private colleges and universities would not be eligible for free tuition.) It should be no surprise that Wall Street made up the top 20 donors list to Mrs. Clinton's campaign. After all, the government would want to borrow the money needed to foot the tuition bill from Wall Street banks. So why stop free tuition at public colleges only? According to the College Board, the average cost of tuition for the 2016–2017 school year was $33,480 at private colleges, $9,650 for state residents at a public college.[28] Lending money to students who attend private colleges is more lucrative to Wall Street than servicing government-backed loans to students attending public colleges. Graduates of private colleges leave school with an average debt of $34,000 while graduates of public colleges carry a debt load of $27,000. (The average 2016 college graduate has $37,172 in student loan debt.[29]) College for all, even if tuition must be paid by students, would be a big moneymaker for Wall Street.

The student loan industry isn't just for banks anymore. Students may now borrow directly from the U.S. Department of Education. But the DOE is not loaning money to help the student get an affordable college education. They lend money to make money, period. The Department of Education borrows money from the U.S. Treasury at low-interest rates and lends to students at a much higher rate. The Congressional Budget Office (CBO) reported the DOE made a profit of $41.3 billion on student loans during 2013. To put that number in perspective, for the fiscal year 2012, Exxon Mobil earned $44.9

billion while Apple made $41.9 billion. Now we can see why the federal government wants everyone to attend college. It's not to pull us out of poverty but to put us in debt. Currently, over 44 million college graduates owe nearly $1.3 trillion in student loan debt. That works out to about $29,500 per graduate, and a monthly payment of $350. Now imagine if every American had a college education and the debt that goes with it. The middle class would be completely decimated, and the elite would have the country they want.

A second argument used to support the college for all concept is that a four-year degree is necessary for many of tomorrow's good jobs. Scholars maintain that we must raise the educational attainment of our citizens to meet the knowledge requirements of unknown future jobs. Well, of course, scholars would make such a recommendation. They work for universities and want to ensure an unending supply of customers. But ask the scholars to identify the jobs of the future. Research shows many of today's jobs are the same jobs that will be needed in the future. Forbes Magazine listed the following as the fastest growing jobs through 2020[30]:

1. Registered nurse
2. Retail sales
3. Home health aide
4. Personal care aide

5. Office clerk
6. Food preparation and serving workers
7. Customer service representative
8. Tractor trailer drivers
9. Stock and material laborers
10. University instructor

Technology skills such as software developers, data analysists, and computer programming will no doubt also be important in the future. But just how many will be needed as we move toward a society of artificial intelligence? Smartphones use global positioning systems to chart travel directions. IBM's supercomputer, Watson, grows smarter ever day even to the point of defeating humans in a chess game. Amazon's Alexa adjusts your home's temperature with a single voice command. How soon will it be before artificial intelligence writes computer programs or analyzes data and reports on trends? The overriding question with future jobs is not one of education or training. Rather, what is the best and most effective way to gain work-related skills? A four-year college degree is not a one size fits all answer. It is just one of a variety of paths that could lead to fulfilling future specialized job requirements.

Another argument for college for all is it is needed to drive innovation and change. The belief is that college, and its artificial worldly environment will prepare individuals to solve real world problems. But that is not really the case. College offers students many safety nets for failure – there is no real consequence for failure (except a poor grade). The real world offers no such safety nets. Mistakes cost money, jobs, and even lives. Innovation comes from addressing real problems in a real environment; it's that simple. College and innovation may not be compatible.

But there is one final problem with college for all – a very fundamental problem that cannot be ignored. America's public K-12 educational system does not prepare students for success in college. America graduates only about 82 percent of all high school students. Furthermore, according to *U.S. News and World Report,* only about 37 percent of high school graduates are equipped for college level math and reading.[31] Illiteracy in the United States remains a serious problem. It has been estimated that:[32]

- Some 63 million adults read between a sixth grade and eighth-grade level.
- Just 12 percent of adults are proficient readers.
- 30 million adults read below a fifth-grade level.
- 44 million adults read at a very basic level.
- 32 million adults cannot read.

- 19 percent of all high school graduates cannot read.

And what about those students who do attend college? A study of students entering college in fall 2010 by the *National Student Clearinghouse Research Center* found that by June 2016, six years of enrollment, just 54.8 percent of students had graduated.[33] As we shall learn, these results are not unexpected.

Education Unions Control Public Education

While education union leaders are not as affluent as Wall Street bankers, they have been very successful at buying political votes. The unions have enormous control over politicians. As George Carlin suggested, union leaders do not want well-informed and well-educated people interfering with the public education process. Union leaders want happy members and lots of them. More members bring union leadership more political power and higher salaries for the leadership. For example, the current president of the United Federation of Teachers, which represents New York City, earns roughly $280,000 per year. That is just under four times higher than the average New York City teachers' salary. The UFT contributed about $5 million to politicians in 2014 and $0 on improving education. In the same year, the president of the National

American Federation of Teachers was paid more than $557,000.

The relationship between union leader salaries and the number of members influences the causes promoted by the education unions. For example, education unions are against charter schools, school choice, and vouchers because they would reduce membership numbers in the union. How? Charter schools are run by private entities. Unlike state government run schools, teachers at charter schools are not required to pay dues to a state or national union as a condition of employment. The same is true for private and religious schools. More school choice options for kids would reduce big union membership, its power, and the salaries of its leaders.

Education unions often refer to the familiar battle cry of "putting kids first," but don't you believe it. The education unions represent teachers and not students. As a former president of the UFT, put it, *"When schoolchildren start paying union dues, that's when I'll start representing the interests of schoolchildren."* Teacher interests are different than student interests. Teachers have been indoctrinated to believe they have the right to tenure (lifetime job regardless of performance), salary based on seniority, short days, long holidays, and the opportunity to retire early at 55 with a lifetime pension and full health benefits. What employee wouldn't want these benefits? But these benefits are just that, benefits. They have nothing to do getting results in the classroom.

Washington is only too happy to support the wishes of education unions. After all, Washington is owned by Wall Street. And Wall Street will use any patsy to protect their interests. Think about this for a moment. Washington loves to remind us that "education is the only path out of poverty." Such slogans are meant to deflect the issues surrounding poverty away from Wall Street and place them on a government institution that no one really believes can ever be totally successful. No doubt that education can pull some out of poverty, but the most effective way to end poverty is through well-paying jobs. To create well-paying jobs Wall Street would have to sanction wage increases over double digit corporate profits. Reducing corporate profits would mean less new money to the already super wealthy. That's not what Wall Street wants. They don't want to share America's wealth with you. And they don't want you to know that education is not the only answer to poverty. *"You know what they want? Obedient workers - people who are just smart enough to run the machines and do the paperwork but just dumb enough to passively accept all these increasingly shittier jobs with the lower pay, the longer hours, reduced benefits, the end of overtime and the vanishing pension that disappears the minute you go to collect it."[34]* And they want you to think that the poverty problem can only be fixed through education.

Public school unions are not the only ones controlling education. At the university level, the American Association of University Professors (AAUP) has successfully given professors total control over courses and course content. AAUP developed a set of guidelines that all universities adhere to. The Statement of Principles on Academic Freedom and Tenure is woven into the labor agreement between the university and the professors. This legally binding contract states that professors have complete freedom to teach any topic, any idea, using any materials they choose. In other words, individual professors are left to teach what they want. This means that two students attending the same university, taking the same course taught by two different professors could be exposed to two different sets of curriculum content.

Education Agenda Controlled by Elite

You might be tempted to believe that kindergarten in the United States began as the first step toward improving academic achievement. Sounds good but it's not quite right. Public kindergartens took off in large cities during the 1870s. After the Civil War, the United States accepted a multitude of immigrants from Southern and Eastern Europe. The education elite viewed these immigrants, mostly from Italy, Poland, and Greece as less intelligent and industrious than previous immigrants from Western Europe, namely Germany and England. Kindergartens were invented as a way of teaching social and good citizenship skills to the new immigrants. The curriculum concentrated on the teaching of morality, good virtues, and habits of cleanliness and hygiene.[35] Kindergarten was seen as a way to Americanize immigrant children by reducing the amount of time they had to interact with their "uneducated and lazy" parents and immoral influences found on urban street corners.

Those efforts were just the beginning of a century-long effort to use education as a tool to indoctrinate children with specific and new social behaviors having little to do with academics but everything to do with creating obedient workers and citizens. Consider the following instances.

1. 1928. American Association for the Advancement of Science meeting. A teacher was invited to participate alongside education's elite professors such as John Dewey, Edward Thorndike and other members of the Progressive Education movement. The teacher, O.A. Nelson gave the following testimony regarding the meeting to the *National Educator* in 1979:*"I know from personal experience what I am talking about.*

In December 1928, I was asked to talk to the American Association for the Advancement of Science. On December 27th, naïve and inexperienced, I agreed. I had done some special work in teaching functional physics in high school. That was to be my topic. The next day, the 28th, a Dr. Ziegler asked me if I would attend a special educational meeting in his room after the AAAS meeting. We met from 10 o'clock (p.m.) until after 2:30 a.m. We were 13 at the meeting. Two things caused Dr. Ziegler, who was Chairman of the Educational Committee of the Council on Foreign Relations, to ask me to attend... my talk on the teaching of functional physics in high school, and the fact that I was a member of a group known as the Progressive Educators of America, which was nothing but a Communist front. I thought the word "progressive" meant progress for better schools. Eleven of those attending the meeting were leaders in education. Drs. John Dewey and Edward Thorndike, from Columbia University, were there, and the others were of equal rank. I checked later and found that ALL were paid members of the Communist Party of Russia. I was classified as a member of the Party, but I did not know it at the time. The sole work of the group was to destroy our schools! We spent one hour and forty-five minutes discussing the so-called Modern Math. At one point I objected because there was too much memory work, and math is reasoning; not memory. Dr. Ziegler turned to me and said, 'Nelson, wake up! That is what we want... a math that the pupils cannot apply to life situations when they get out of school!' That math was not introduced until much later, as those present thought it was too radical a change. A milder course by Dr. Breckner was substituted but it was also worthless, as far as understanding math was concerned. The radical change was introduced in 1952. It was the one we are using now. So, if pupils come out of high school now, not knowing any math, don't blame them. The results are supposed to be worthless."

2. 1930s. Progressive education professors changed how reading was taught in America's school. Since the creation of the alphabet, civilizations have used phonics (each letter of the alphabet represents a unique sound) to teach reading. The ancient Greeks and Romans used phonics. The American colonies created a phonics textbook, *New England Primer*, back in 1690. Phonics was used to teach reading in America without question

until the 1890s when John Dewey began a movement to change education from intellectual training to conditioning students to be obedient, conformist, non-thinkers. One of his disciples William Gray, dean of the University of Chicago's School of Education, convinced the National Education Association that phonics instruction should be replaced with the look-say technique. (Look-say involves memorizing a whole word without recognizing the individual sounds of letters in the word. Committing the word to memory through repetition is a form of behavior conditioning.) In 1930 Scott Foresman published Gray's new reader, *Dick and Jane*. These readers, or primers, soon gained dominance in American elementary schools. Mr. Gray earned millions in royalties from the sale of the textbooks. Meanwhile, by the mid-1930s, parents began complaining their children could not read. Remedial reading classes and dyslexia were born. (As a point of reference to show the distinction between phonics and look-say, think of the work of an architect. For example, when designing a new bridge one would hope that the architect understands the smallest components that constitute the structure of a sound bridge. Such an architect could build functionally sound bridges in any topography. But an architect who designs a bridge just based on the memory of a bridge previously seen does so without understanding what makes a bridge functional. You wouldn't want to cross that bridge.)

3. 1932. The publication of, *DARE THE SCHOOL BUILD A NEW SOCIAL ORDER* written by Professor George Counts of Columbia University Teachers College. Counts had traveled to Russia many times and was convinced that the Soviet Communist education system was the best system in the world. Counts was a member of a commission examining the place of social studies in the American curriculum.[36] Without focusing on the recommendations, I would simply like to point out the mindset of the commission as it set the tone for all recommendations. In its report, the Commission states what it feels are its obligations. I list two to shed light on their thinking.

- *"The Commission could not limit itself to a survey of textbooks, curricula, methods of instruction, and schemes of examination, but was impelled to consider the condition and prospects of the American people as a part of Western civilization now merging into a world order."*

- *"The Commission was also driven to this broader conception of its task by the obvious fact that American civilization, in common with Western civilization, is passing through one of the great critical ages of history, is modifying its traditional faith in economic individualism, and is embarking upon vast experiments in social planning and control which call for large-scale co-operation on the part of the people."* It is clear that the commission was more concerned with training children to be citizens of the world rather than understanding the history of America.

4. 1949. Ralph Tyler, professor and chair of the department of education at the University of Chicago published *Basic Principals of Curriculum and Instruction.* The following short excerpt conveys his education philosophy. *"Since the real purpose of education is not to have the instructor perform certain activities but to bring about significant changes in the student's pattern of behavior, it becomes important to recognize that any statement of the objective... should be a statement of changes to take place in the student."* In other words, Tyler said education is not about academic prowess but about programming behaviors. This book is still in

use today in many university education programs.

5. 1955. Rudolf Flesch published *Why Johnny Can't Read: And What You Can Do about It.* In his book, Flesch argues the look-say method of teaching reading is a complete failure. The education elite fought back through Arthur Gates, a professor at Columbia University, trying to discredit Flesch. Gates was also the editor of a widely used basal reader published by the Macmillan Company. Like Gray, Gates was making millions of dollars promoting the look-say method. Nothing changed. The look-say method continued to be used in schools all over America.

6. 1955. Nila B. Smith, professor of education at New York University wrote the following excerpt published in the NEA Journal, "*In the future, reading instruction must concern itself with much more than pedagogy. It must mesh more directly with the gears of vital social problems.*" The purpose of reading is to solve social problems? No, learning to read should stand on its own legs for the singular purpose of developing literate individuals. Literate adult citizens can then determine for themselves what societal problems need to be addressed and how best to tackle them.

7. 1956. Benjamin Bloom published *Taxonomy of Educational Objectives: The Classification of Educational Goals.* The taxonomy was used to break down children's actions into units of behavior which could be identified, measured, and changed. This deconstructing of the child was intended to separate children from their natural identity. The child could then be programmed by schools into an individual more desirable by society. The fictional character Jason Bourne would serve as an example of Bloom's taxonomy if it were possible to implement to its fullest extent.

8. 1967. Jeanne Chall, a professor at Harvard Graduate School of Education published, *Learning to Read: The Great Debate.* In her book, Chall presented several years of extensive research studies showing that phonics-based instruction produced more proficient readers whereas, look-say instruction produced many students with reading difficulties. The education elites politely called her work ill-conceived, unrespectable, and other disapproving criticisms. They effectively silenced her warnings.

9. 1968. Professor John Goodlad, dean at UCLA's School of Education, publishes an article *"Learning and Teaching in the Future"*

in the National Education Association's journal TODAY'S EDUCATION. One passage reads: *"The most controversial issues of the twenty-first century will pertain to the ends and means of modifying human behavior and who shall determine them. The first educational question will not be 'what knowledge is of the most worth?' but 'what kinds of human beings do we wish to produce?"*

10. 1976. The president of the National Education Association gave a speech to NEA members and declared, *"First, we will help all of our people understand that school is a concept and not a place. We will not confuse 'schooling' with education."*

11. 1973. Chester M. Pierce, a professor of the department of educational psychiatry, Harvard University states during an education seminar in Denver, *"Every child in America entering school at the age of five is insane because he comes to school with certain allegiances toward our Founding Fathers, toward his parents, toward our elected officials, toward a belief in a supernatural being, and toward the sovereignty of this nation as a separate entity. It's up to you, teachers, to make all these sick children well*

by creating the international child of the future."

12. 1977. Mary Jo Bane, associate professor of education, Harvard Graduate School of Education. Future Assistant Secretary of Administration for Children and Families at the US Department of Health and Human Services, 1993-1996 states, *"We really don't know how to raise children. If we want to talk about the equality of opportunity for children, then the fact that children are raised in families means there's no equality, we must take them away from families and communally raise them."*

13. 1981. William H. Seawell, professor of education, University of Virginia states, *"We must focus on creating citizens for the good of society, public schools promote civic rather than individual pursuit. Each child belongs to the state."*

14. 1984. U.S. Senator Peter Hoagland from Nebraska declares, *"Fundamental, Bible - believing people do not have the right to indoctrinate their children in their religious beliefs because we, the state, are preparing them for the year 2000, when America will be part of a one-word global society and their children will not fit in. The reason we have to regulate church schools is that children that*

are not trained in state-controlled schools will not fit in."

15. 2005. The National Center for Policy Analysis shed light on a new mathematics textbook designed to teach social justice through mathematics. Chapter topics included topics such as *Sweatshop Accounting, Multicultural Math, Racial Profiling, Environmental Racism and Home Buying While Brown or Black*. The book, titled, *Rethinking Mathematics: Teaching Social Justice by the Numbers*.

16. 2015. U.S. Education Secretary makes following comments at a youth violence summit. *"One idea that I threw out ... is this idea of public boarding schools. That's a little bit of a different idea, a controversial idea." "But the question is — do we have some children where there's not a mom, there's not a dad, there's not a grandma, there's just nobody at home? There's just certain kids we should have 24/7 to really create a safe environment and give them a chance to be successful."*

17. September 2016. First Lady Michelle Obama declares, *"the choice in this election is about who will have the power to shape our children for the next four years of their lives."*

How Congress Controls Education

Let's start with a brief history of the federal government's influence on education.

1. Land Ordinance of 1785. Required every township in the Northwest to set aside a plot of land for construction of a public school.
2. 1847. Congress gave away 77 million acres of land to states to be used for public education.
3. 1862, Morrill Act. Congress gave public lands to states for the purpose of establishing at least one college for the teaching of agriculture, mechanic arts, and industrial education.
4. 1867. The federal Office of Education was established to collect data on effective teaching.
5. 1890, the second Morrill Act. Congress gave the Office of Education responsibility for supporting public land-grant colleges.
6. 1917. Congress passed the Smith-Hughes Act to promote vocational schools
7. 1939 - 1950. American Council on Education established a National Teachers' Examination to ensure all teachers possessed basic literacy, numeracy, and communication skills. The university schools' of education fought these tests until they died in 1950.

8. 1944. GI bill provided financial assistance for post-secondary studies for soldiers returning from World War II.
9. 1946, The George-Barden Act gave funding for agricultural, industrial and home economics courses in high schools.
10. 1965, Elementary and Secondary Education Act. Established funding to public and private schools to develop education programs to disadvantaged students.
11. 1973, Section 504 of the Rehabilitation Act. Eliminated discrimination against disabled students.
12. 1980. Federal Department of Education as a cabinet position was established.
13. 1983. The Federal government transferred responsibility for administering the nation's report card, NAEP to the Educational Testing Service.
14. 1989-1992. The Indian Education Bill of Rights was enacted; work began on creating national education standards.
15. 2001-2008 – Congress authorized No Child Left Behind.
16. 2009. Common Core Standards adopted.
17. 2015, Every Student Succeeds Act passed.

Serious interventions in public education began in the 1960s. From 1965-1969, Michigan State University designed a new teacher preparation program. It was funded by U.S. Department of Health, Education, and Welfare and called *The Behavioral Science Teacher Education Program* (BSTEP).[37] The program had three major goals.

1. Development of a new kind of elementary school teacher, one who functions as a social change agent. (The teacher will have the ability to relate with, manipulate, and evaluate student behavior. Not learning, just social behaviors.)
2. Student teachers would be informed on non-Western thought and values.
3. Establish a new laboratory and clinical base from the behavioral sciences.

BSTEP called for shifting the focus of education away from academics and onto systemic student behaviors, feelings, emotions, and role playing – programming children to behave in a similar manner. BSTEP became the standard used by almost all teacher-training schools of education. Teachers have been trained to become technicians, implementers of teacher proof curriculum that require mandated outcomes as verified through national standardized tests.

But it was in the 1990s when the federal government really took control of the curriculum used in public schools. In 1994, Congress passed the Goals 2000 Educate America Act, the School-to-

Work Opportunities Act (STW), and the reauthorization of the Elementary and Secondary Education Act (ESEA). These three laws work in concert to influence curriculum. Goals 2000 implies that objectives in the law are voluntary but the ESEA law specifies that if a state (and school district) do not comply with Goals 2000, all federal funds will be withheld. Federal funds account for about nine percent of local education funding. Nine percent may not sound like much but consider that since 1980, the federal government has spent $1.5 trillion on education. That kind of money buys a lot of influence.

The federal government uses money as the carrot to drive state curriculums. The Department of Education (DOE) awards discretionary grants that drive state governments to adopt federally approved standards and assessments. States that comply with DOE wishes get paid. This is how the DOE circumvents the U.S. Constitution. The Tenth Amendment of the Constitution states that any power not given to the federal government is given to the states.

Money isn't the only control exercised by the federal government. To receive federal funds, the states must sign an agreement to share student academic data with the U.S. Department of Education using the State Longitudinal Data System (SLDS). Data collected includes the following:

religious affiliation, fingerprints, healthcare history, family income range, disciplinary record, family voting status, handwriting samples, DNA sequence, and if available retina and iris scans, voice prints, and facial characteristics. Do you get the feeling that the U.S. Department of Education is interested in something other than student academic success? You might be right. Why would the Department of Education need student DNA, fingerprints, family voting history, or other personal data? The argument used by the DOE is this data is needed to create computerized, personalized, and learning experiences. Computer software would use student data to design lessons based on the students' non-cognitive skills such as current mindset and emotional status. But is that claim true? Shane Vander Hart of Kansans Against Common Core doesn't believe so. *"Federal involvement in education is about control, not education. The partnership between the federal departments of Labor and Education to further the development of fully functioning statewide birth-to-adulthood databases on citizens, and commonality of standards and testing across the country is reshaping the nation. It will result, as intended, in only people whose education they can control getting jobs, getting into college, and getting into the military. It's a tool of control, not a tool of education."*[38]

If you don't want to believe that listen to what United States Congressmen Jason Chaffetz from Utah had to say after participating in a 2015 U.S. Department of Education information security review. *"Almost half of the population of the United States of America has their personal information sitting in this database, which is not secure."* Granted, the House Committee was only investigating data security, but what they discovered suggests the Department of Education is not interested in student academic success. Here is what Congressman Chaffetz found[39]:

- The Department of Education has at least 139 million unique social security numbers in its Central Processing System (CPS).
- Reminiscent of Office of Personnel Management's (OPM) dangerous behavior, DOE is not heeding repeat warnings from the Inspector General (IG) that their information systems are vulnerable to security threats.
- The Department scored NEGATIVE 14 percent on the Office of Management and Budget (OMB) CyberSprint for total users using strong authentication.
- The Department of Education received an "F" on the Federal Information Technology Reform Act (FITARA) scorecard.
- The Department of Education maintains 184 information systems.

- 120 of the information systems are managed by outside contractors.
- 29 of the information systems are valued by the (OMB) as "high asset."
- The IG penetrated DOE systems completely undetected by both the chief information officer and contractor.

The U.S. Department of Education is embarking on a mission to collect massive amounts of personal student data yet this sensitive information is not protected. It is readily available to third party vendors and anyone curious enough to tap into their data banks. Again, does this sound like the DOE is interested in student academic achievement? The data collected by the department has no academic value. Its only value is to track the behaviors of citizens from the cradle to the grave.

Education Curriculum Controlled by University

Washington and Wall Street may control the amount of funding available for all education programs from pre-school through graduate school, but higher education controls what is taught when it is taught, and how much is taught. Knowledge is the currency of the university. Just like Wall Street decides who gets wealthy, universities decide who gets access to knowledge. By knowledge, I do not imply the things you learned in elementary, high school or even college. What you gained from those experiences was a tool bag filled with instruments designed to help you solve the very simplest of problems. Your bag contains no tools to help you unravel complex and complicated questions. That is by design. If the average American was taught to be an independent and critical thinker, the role and status of the university would be diminished. Imagine a land where most citizens were prepared for the workforce, public discourse on social issues, and ready to participate in public office without the need for college. Professors, don't fret. This won't happen. You have legions of graduates who will continue to carry your banner. You control them. You control knowledge distribution. The following represent some examples of how the education elite have controlled American education throughout the decades.

The university maintains control in very subtle ways that might go unnoticed to the outside observer. Nevertheless, the university elite calls the shots. They control who gets into college and who doesn't. They control the university curriculum. The university elite establishes course content, textbooks to be used, and how important a topic is in the overall study in a chosen field. But how does this control really affect you?

Let's begin by weighing the number of graduates against the number of available jobs. The business of the university is to sell classes and acquire sizable federal grants for questionable research projects. The university does not exist to give you marketable employment skills or a job on Wall Street. In fact, according to the Bureau of Labor Statistics (BLS), only 27 percent of jobs in the U.S. require at least an associate degree. But it gets worse. The BLS projections show the economy will create 50.6 million job openings by 2022 and only 27.1 percent will require college degrees.[40]

The spring of 2014 saw 1,869,814 bachelor degrees confirmed in the United States. Business majors led the way with 19,2 percent of all degrees followed by the humanities granting 15.5 percent, behavioral sciences with 15.5 percent, computer sciences and engineering at 8.8 percent, natural sciences and math at 8.3 percent, education with 5.3 percent. The most recent study of job placement by the U.S. Census Bureau shows that 75 percent of engineer graduates are likely to find jobs that require a bachelor's degree, but not necessarily a job in engineering.[41] About 42 percent of social science, business, liberal arts, and communication graduates will find work in a job that requires a bachelor's degree, but not necessarily in their field of study. Only a third of graduates with a degree in hospitality will find work in a field that requires a bachelor's degree. The Census Bureau also found that graduates with jobs unrelated to their college major earn less money than graduates with jobs in their field of study. What do these numbers really mean? Higher education does not do enough for most students to prepare them for entry-level work in their field of study. There is a huge disconnect between students education plans and their career plans.

College presidents typically claim the mission of higher education is to prepare students for life. They very rarely use the words, *work, job,* or *career.* Instead, they use phrases like *intellectual curiosity,* the *enlightenment of the mind,* and *probing the mysterious realms of thought* when they talk about the purpose of college. And for a good reason. College students are required to take roughly 40 to 60 percent of their classes outside of their major. If it wasn't for these universal general liberal arts requirements, students could complete their degree in less than four years. For the university, less time to complete a degree equals less overall revenue. Remember, the university is in the business of selling classes. And like all businesses, the best and cheapest way to increase revenue is to sell more products to returning customers. In other words, keeping students enrolled for as long as they can. Sell them classes they don't need or want.

Now perhaps some may say that a liberal arts education produces better thinking citizens. Individuals who have studied Descartes, Plato, and Socrates, who have read Shakespeare, Tolstoy, and Poe must be smarter than citizens who have not attended college. Right? Not so fast. Behind Canada, the United States has the highest percentage of college graduates in the world. Yet according to the Program for the International Assessment of Adult Competencies (PIAAC), which assesses the cognitive skills of adults in three areas—literacy, numeracy, and problem-solving - we are not number two in smarts. On the literacy scale, the United States came in at number 13 with five countries behind us and five countries tied with the U.S. In numeracy, the United States came in at number 19 with two countries lower and two countries tied with the U.S. On problem-solving, the United States finished at number 15 with four other countries tied with the U.S.

So why aren't Americans smarter, especially college graduates? There are several possible reasons. First, liberal arts classes are standalone courses. They are not connected to each other or to other liberal art subject matter. Courses provide the student with no more than a very rudimentary introduction to one small piece of the universe. So are we to believe that one class in any one liberal art subject will help students learn the meaning of life? Become a better citizen? Develop an enlightened mind? I don't think so. A three credit liberal arts course usually includes about 42 hours of classroom time spread over a 15-week timeline. Not enough time to even begin to scratch the surface of each topic let alone how that topic fits into the bigger picture of mankind. (Notice I chose the words *class time* rather than *instruction* because many of the required liberal arts classes are taught in a 300 seat theater style lecture hall by a 22-year grad student who is far from being a knowledgeable instructor in the field.)

A second possible reason for a poor liberal arts global performance is college students are forced to take an array of liberal art classes before they are permitted to pursue the courses in their major. When you compel individuals, especially teenagers, to comply with seemingly senseless directives, you create resentment. Students take the required liberal arts classes not to seek knowledge and enlightenment, but simply to meet an unpleasant obligation necessary to gain the degree. For many, the required liberal arts class are nothing more than a checkmark on the degree guidelines checklist.

Now let's take a look at what really constitutes a college degree. Generally speaking, students must complete at least 120 credits, or around 40 courses, to receive a bachelor's degree. In many cases, half or more of the 120 credits must come from studies outside the major field of study. For example, typical non-major courses for a bachelor's degree in any field include the following general education liberal arts classes:

- 3 credits of western civilization,
- 8 credits of natural sciences,
- 6 credits written communications,
- 3 credits oral communications,
- 3 credits college algebra,
- 3 credits in statistics,
- 3 credits of literature,
- 3 credits of arts,
- 3 credits in philosophy,
- 3 credits in psychology or sociology,
- 3 credits foreign language,
- 6 credits in physical education, and
- 3 to 6 credits in information technology.

The following are a few examples of typically required courses for the major field of study.

Accounting Major Requirements

- 54 total credits in major course work

Elementary Teacher Education Major Requirements

- 42 total credits in major course work, mostly instructional multi-subject methods courses, includes student teaching

Biology Major Requirements

- 54 total credits in major course work

Electrical Engineering Admin Major Requirements

- 47 to 64 total credits in electrical engineering major coursework

The basic general liberal arts education requirements for any field of study are nothing more than an assembly line process where every student tolerates the same repetitive and dull classes that were taught for the last 50 years. The same classes that should have been taught and mastered in high school. Honestly, should college students be required to take gym classes? English composition? An art class? You get the point. This mass production of general education courses is in place for one reason, and one reason only – to produce revenue for the university. They offer no value to the student as the college requires these very same general education courses to be studied in high school as a basis for university acceptance.

Teacher Education Controlled by Elite

As we have already seen, the elites control the textbooks and materials used in the public school classroom. But they also control something far more important, the education prospective teachers receive. While it is easy and convenient to blame teachers for the failures that exist in public education, most of the negative criticism surrounding school belongs to the university elite. After all, the young adult fresh out of high school can hardly be expected to know what he needs to learn to become an effective teacher. It's not like studying biology, chemistry, or math where the prospective student already has a basic grasp of the content. Teaching is different. Yes, it does involve content expertise, but it also involves knowing how to transfer information to students effectively. That is the tricky part. Unfortunately, many students graduate from teacher education programs not knowing how to teach. And it's not their fault. Their programs of study were designed to leave them confused. It is not uncommon for new teachers to declare that they learned more about teaching in their first couple of years of teaching than they did at the university.

There are numerous reasons for the disconnect between university teacher preparation programs and the reality of the classroom. One of the most bizarre is that the university elite refuses to use the word *training* in regards to teacher education. The word of choice is *preparation*. So what is the big deal about one word that is essentially a synonym of the other? The professors like to say that you train pets, monkeys, animals and not people. Humans prepare. Training, they say, is merely a technical transmission activity void of social and moral viewpoints. What morality is involved with learning to teach a child to read? Either you know how to teach reading, or you don't. The only moral question here is should the university collect tuition for programs that fail to deliver a complete education to their students? Furthermore, the university elite claims the function of teacher education is to launch the prospective teacher on a lifelong path of learning, rather than to teach the valuable skills needed to instruct children effectively. Lifelong learning is a nice ambition, but that decision belongs to the individual and not the university. And when the university fails to give a concrete foundation of knowledge to build on, the pursuit of further knowledge will be built on pillars of sand. One final note just to underscore the denial of the word training. The Thomas B. Fordham Institute conducted a survey of education professors in 2012 and found that just 37 percent believed it was their job to train teachers how to maintain discipline and order in a classroom. The other 63 percent said it was not their job to be a trainer of teachers.[42]

Teacher education programs rely on classes known as method courses. An outsider might think that a methods course is all about learning the best methods to teach a particular subject. That opinion would be wrong. According to a report on teacher education programs by the American Educational Research Association (AERA), college of education professors view method courses as "*A methods course is seldom defined as a class that transmits information about methods of instruction and ends with a final exam. They are seen as complex sites in which instructors work simultaneously with prospective teachers on beliefs, teaching practices and creation of identities—their students' and their own.*"[43] Warm fuzzies cannot replace knowledge. The university graduates new teachers, typically 21 or 22 years of age, knowing they have been deprived of experiencing teaching methods that work and are based on solid research.

New teachers generally get very little practical training before they enter the classroom. The college elite designed teacher education programs that way. The elite wants education to be a profession, but they do not want to put actual work into achieving that goal. Yes, they have done a tremendous job of pretending to be professional and in selling professionalism, but when you take a deep dive, you discover the hoax. First, let's look at the presentation of education classes within the college. The courses are taught by a multitude of instructors. Some are professors who haven't set foot in a classroom in 30 years, others are graduate students who have never been employed in public education, and some are associate professors with a mix of public education and college teaching. All have different beliefs as to what constitutes good teaching. The 19, 20, and 21-

year-old students are often left conflicted about the messages they receive from a Goldilocks array of university instructors. When these students are placed in public schools for short observational studies they often find more conflict between the college instructor and what they see in the school setting. Many times there is a huge disconnect between what the college is teaching and what the public school wants. The college elite believes it is their role to tell the public school what they need and not the other way around.

The big finale in a teacher education program is student teaching. At the end of their studies, prospective teachers are assigned placement in a public school setting for a time of eight to 16 weeks, depending on the college and state requirements. The public school assigns the prospective teacher to a cooperating teacher, a teacher who volunteers to take on a student teacher. Not all cooperating teachers are cooperative. Some cooperating teachers introduce the student teacher to the class and then retire to the teachers' lounge for the rest of the semester. Others require the student teacher to correct papers, make photocopies and take all lunch, bus, and other duties in place of the cooperating teacher. And still other cooperating teachers require the student teacher to just sit in the back of the room and observe. They are afraid to let the student teacher teach because they might make mistakes for which the cooperating

117

teacher will be blamed. There are other unpleasant scenarios that could take place. The cooperating teacher just doesn't like the student teacher or vice versa, a basic difference of philosophies on discipline, etc. You get the point.

By now you might be asking about the university's role in student teaching. The university rarely investigates the school or cooperating teachers to discover if they are a good fit for the universities teachings. Universities usually send out a request to public schools to determine interests in student teachers. If the interests are low, the university will place as many student teachers within one school district as possible. If the interest is high, the university will spread the student teachers over a wide geographic area. (Student teachers placed in urban schools experience a different reality than those place in suburban schools.) And in some cases, when interest is very low the university will ask the student teacher to find their own public school placement. After the student teacher is placed in a school setting, they are assigned a field supervisor from the university. The supervisor will not be a tenured professor of education, or an associate professor, and probably not even an assistant professor. More than likely, the field supervisor will be someone the student teacher has never met like a Ph.D. student (who receives college credits for the assignment), an adjunct instructor, or someone hired by the university for the sole purpose of supervising student teachers. In almost all cases the field supervisor is not an asset to the student teacher because they lack any real context. They don't know the student teacher, the public school, or what the college has taught the student teacher. And they visit the student teacher for 45 to 60 minutes once or twice during the semester.

It wasn't always this way. Back in the 19th century, when university schools of education were created, teacher education programs were based on the medical model of training doctors. Potential teachers studied subject matter and were tested on their knowledge prior to receiving a job offer. At the beginning of the 20th century, college of education professors became jealous of the professionalism of medical and law schools. Both professions trained candidates through graduate schools. Furthermore, both professions controlled the licensing of their professionals. The education elites wanted the same thing and created the Graduate School of Education (GSE). The GSE's were staffed with professors of education pedagogy. Fancy word but pedagogy basically means the art or work of a teacher. Unfortunately, pedagogy does not include mastery of subject matter.

Just as important, the education elites wanted control over the certification and licensing of teachers. The creation of graduate schools of education gave the university elite the leverage they needed to gain control. State departments of education were convinced to replace subject matter exams as a qualification for teacher certification with standards established by the graduate school of education. Standards were considered met with a bachelor degree granted from a teacher preparation college program.

The college elite were not the only ones interested in controlling licensing of teachers. In 1946, the NEA created a commission known as the National Commission on Teacher Education and Professional Standards. TEPS, as it was known, set out to create its own set of professional standards to control entry into the teaching profession. NEA sold the project to the public as a measure to protect children from incompetent teachers. Their members, however, were told the commission's work was to protect the members of NEA from unfair competition from untrained people - as determined by TEPS. In other words, the NEA was trying to wrestle teacher certification control away from graduate schools of education to grow NEA membership.

Teachers are not the only victims of poor university training. Principals and superintendents often are not prepared for their role in education. And again, it is not their fault. These administrators are prepared at the same graduate schools of education that control teacher preparation. Typically, most states require a master degree in education administration as the basic requirement to qualify as a principal and superintendent of schools. Although no state requires a doctorate of education (Ed.D.) for employment as a superintendent, many school districts do. And similar to teacher preparation programs, master and doctorate coursework is largely unrelated to either of the positions. Clinical and executive coaching opportunities are not part of the programs. Typical master programs require 10 courses such as:

1. Educational Leadership
2. Curriculum and Instructional Leadership
3. Administration of School Personnel
4. Public School Law
5. Public School Finance
6. Technology Leadership
7. Educational Organization and Administration
8. Leading Change
9. Communications in Educational Leadership
10. Supervision and Professional Development

Typical doctorate requirements include possession of master degree and 10 courses such as;
1. Foundations of Teaching and Learning

2. Introduction to Education, Culture, and Society
3. Introductory Statistics for Educational Research
4. Qualitative Modes of Inquiry
5. Current Issues in Educational Policy
6. Ethical Educational Leadership
7. Organizational Leadership
8. Educational Technology Foundation
9. Curriculum Planning and Design
10. Educational Reform

The courses may sound as if they may have some relevance to leadership, but most provide no value to the job of principal and superintendent. The principal and superintendent positions are two of the most misunderstood jobs in America. Let's start with the principal. Too many people, including some principals and superintendents, think the role is to teach teachers how to teach or to discipline students. If that were the case, which is not, the university would have failed again as they provide no training in these areas. When you think of a principal you should think of general manager of a factory or the store manager of a large retail store because their roles are similar. The principal is responsible for the coordination of the day-to-day activities of the school including the hiring of staff, budgeting, purchasing supplies, emergency drills, evaluating staff performance, and contributing to a healthy school environment. And yes, student discipline sneaks into the realm of responsibilities mostly because teachers, who are responsible for classroom discipline, are not trained at the university on how to maintain discipline. Yet with these responsibilities the principal receives very little, if any training, from the university in the areas of responsibility. Take building or facility management for example. Neither the principal nor superintendent receives any training about things like HVAC, structural repairs, roofing materials, fire barriers, etc. This is just one of several reasons why school buildings across America are falling apart. School administrators don't know what they should know about maintaining facilities.

Contract negotiations is a vital element in any general manager's job, yet school administrators haven't a clue as for how to negotiate. You can see this every August when teachers threaten to strike because they don't have a contract. Schools continually overspend on supplies and services because they don't know any better.

And then there is finance. At best a school superintendent will have taken one course in school budgets. That is not enough. The superintendent of schools is the CEO of the town's largest employer. The superintendent needs to have a deep understanding of finance including, budgeting, bonds, tax rates, municipal home and commercial real estate assessments, bank interest rates, capital improvements, etc. The superintendent is not prepared to handle the financial aspects of leadership. And that's just the way the university elite want it - school administrators who don't fully understand their role will look to the university for curriculum and policy guidance. And as long as the public blames school administrators and teachers for America's failing schools, the university schools of education will control the education agenda and what your child learns, or doesn't learn.

Summary

Our politicians and the media seem to think that college for all adults is a good thing. Yet, when surveyed just 38 percent of recent college graduates (2006 to 2015) think that college was worth the cost.[44] That's a fairly accurate and sad commentary on the state of higher education in the United States. It also exposes disconnect between the average American and the elite who tell us what we should do. But the news is even grimmer. Another Gallup Poll found only 20 percent of U.S. workers believe their jobs utilize their talents and education.[45] Staying with Gallup, another poll found that barely one in ten corporate leaders feel that a college education provides graduates with the skills and proficiencies that their business needs.[46] So there you have it.

Recent college graduates, workers, and business leaders all agree that a college education not the solution to America's workplace needs.

But the wishes of the ordinary American don't count. The controlling elites want followers, people who will do what they are told. The elites place a large debt on the middle class with their callous and self-serving tactics. We know that one aspect of education, illiteracy, has a negative effect on our economy. In terms of productivity, it has been estimated that adult non-readers costs America $225 billion each year.[47] Likewise, adults who lack basic reading skills cost the health care system $100 billion annually. The elites don't pay for that loss, you and I do.

How Do We Get Control

Proposal 1: Deferred Tuition

Purchasing a college degree should be treated the same as any other service. The college gets paid at the time the degree is completed. You don't pay your barber before the haircut, tip the waiter before the meal, or pay the undertaker before the body is buried. Why should college be any different? Pay after graduation with zero percent interest loans. After all, if the government wants everyone to attend college the least they could do is provide interest-free loans.

Proposal 2: Eliminate Liberal Arts Requirements

It's time to make college both affordable and relevant to employment within the field of study. One way to achieve both goals would be to eliminate courses not related to the field of study. Currently, half of all bachelor degree programs consist of non-related liberal arts classes. Let's throw those classes out and replace half of them with additional classes that reflect the needs of employers within the field. Doing so would reduce the number of credits needed to graduate from 120 to 90, or four years to three. The end result- reduced costs and better education.

Proposal 3: Fix Public Education

There are numerous studies that show that if a child cannot read by the end of third grade, the child will never read beyond a very rudimentary level. Two fixes are necessary to correct this problem.

Fix 1. The only subject matter that should be taught in kindergarten through grade 3 is reading. Nothing else. Reading isn't just about communication. Reading improves the ability to focus and concentrate, it helps the brain to analyze and think critically, and it helps improve memory. All of these skills are needed to understand science, math, and history. And the reading that is taught needs to be based on phonics. The look-say method needs to be eliminated from the curriculum.

Fix 2. State governments must change the eligibility of elementary teacher certification to include scientifically proven reading instruction. In the year 2000, the National Reading Panel reported five components necessary for effective reading instruction: phonemic awareness, phonics, fluency, vocabulary, and comprehension.[48] The National Council on Teacher Quality (NCTQ) analyzed elementary teacher preparation programs and found that only 17 percent of colleges taught all five components of effective reading.[49] Furthermore, NCTQ found that 56 percent of the college teacher prep programs addressed no more than two of the essential components. Other findings of the NCTQ:

- Only five of 962 textbooks used in nearly 2,700 different reading courses nationwide rigorously cover the scientific elements of the five essential reading components
- Only five percent of teacher preparation programs provide satisfactory student teaching experiences.
- Just nine percent of university teacher preparation programs actually talk with a student teacher's cooperating teacher.

Currently, many bachelor degree programs in elementary education require just one class in the teaching of reading. That is not enough. Would you go to a dentist who only had one class in repairing cavities? Or a tax accountant who only had one class in tax accounting? Yet it is okay to put teachers who know very little about the teaching of reading into the primary grades in elementary school?

Both of these fixes must come from state governments because we have seen that the university elites will not make the changes necessary to provide teachers with the proper tools to educate our children. These fixes will not go unchallenged, but state governments control the funding state colleges receive. That gives them some leverage. State governments also control certification of teachers. Changing certification requirements would force colleges to adjust their teacher preparation programs.

Proposal 4: Trade Schools

The college for all argument has diminished both the emphasis on alternative places of learning and the diversification of experience. Not every middle class job requires a college education. Plumbers, carpenters, electricians, barbers, chefs are just a few positions that require a different kind of training not found at your local college. In the not too distant past, high school students had choices. They could choose a program of study from college prep, trades, or business. The elites killed these programs in the late 1980s and early 90s claiming they were of no value to society.

It's time to undo the wholesale one size fits all high school. High school should be a time of exploration and discovery. For the first two years of high school expose students to the trades and a variety of real world jobs. Give them opportunities to visit and experience jobs that may interest them. Giving high school students some control over their future career direction would be a good step toward future job satisfaction

State departments of education must make changes. They must take control of education away from the elites and put it in the hands of the local school community.

Proposal 5: Keep Congress out of Education

Do employers really want all employees with the same learning experiences? The diversity of experiences is essential for problem-solving, innovation, and corporate growth. Congress uses federal funds to force states to funnel all students' down the same path. This is bad for students, bad for corporate America, and bad for the economy. Diversity is not just about race, religion, gender, and generations. Employees with different learning experiences and different training provide the perspectives necessary to challenge group think and status quo. A wide assortment of employee experiences and knowledge is necessary for innovation and problem-solving.

Crazy Mark Proposal: No Job, No Tuition

The university would only get paid after graduates completed their first full year of work in their field of study. Professors would soon change their focus from what they think is important to what employers say is important. Hold the university responsible for delivering a worthwhile and valuable product

CHAPTER 4 Foreign Policy

"Tis our true policy to steer clear of permanent alliances with any portion of the foreign world."
- George Washington

"Peace, commerce, and honest friendship with all nations, entangling alliances with none." – Thomas Jefferson

It has been said that those who fail to heed history are doomed to repeat it. When it comes to foreign policy, the United States can't seem to learn from its mistakes. Could it be that all Washington politicians have failed to study history? Could it be that Washington politicians alone have led us down a century long road of global blunders? Or could the Washington politicians have been strong-armed into making decisions that have enriched others? Carroll Quigley, former professor of History at Princeton University, Harvard College, and Georgetown University believed a secret cartel of elitists exists for the purpose of creating a global system of financial control. Quigley spent twenty years researching and writing on this theory. Anthony Sutton, a former Stanford University Hoover Institution Fellow also studied this topic and identified a group called "the Order" as most of its members were also members of the Order of the Skull and Bones of Yale University.

The Order was dominated mainly by two families, the Morgans, and Rockefellers. Quigley claims that the cartel heavily supported the election of President Woodrow Wilson in 1913. You might recall from chapter one in this book that the Federal Reserve System was created and signed into law by Wilson in 1913. As we now know, the Fed is and has been run by Wall Street bankers since the beginning. And as we have already established, the United States involvement in World War I was not one of national security, but rather one that was forced due to publicly announced profit-making loans made to the Allies by Morgan and Wall Street bankers. The Central Powers perceived that Wall Street loans represented a shift of the United States policy from neutrality to a partnership with the Allies. Had Morgan not interfered Wilson may have been able to keep the United States out of WWI saving over 100,000 American lives.

On the surface, Quigley's allegation of global financial imperialism seems far-fetched. And maybe it is. But maybe there is some truth to secret cartels. Let's find out.

Secret Roundtable: Council on Foreign Relations

Quigley claimed that the Morgan and Rockefeller families are part of a cartel that controls worldwide economies.[50] He asserts the families implement their agenda's through roundtables. One such roundtable is the Council on Foreign Relations (CFR) based in New York City. Giving some credence to Quigley's theory, but by no means an indictment of conspiracy, consider the following. Since its beginning in 1921, CFR's members have included:

- 21 U.S. Secretaries of Defense
- 19 Secretaries of Treasury
- 17 Secretaries of State
- 15 CIA Directors
- 10 of 14 President Obama cabinet positions
- Media members include:
  - New York Times
  - Washington Post
  - CNN and other media outlets
- Corporate members include (and many more):
  - Bank of America
  - JP Morgan Chase
  - Morgan Stanley
  - Rockefeller group
  - Soros Fund
  - Exxon Mobile
  - U.S Chamber of Commerce

I am sure that many individuals join the CFR to make business connections, but it is curious that proposed U.S. policy changes appear in the CFR magazine *Foreign Affairs* prior to passage or mass publication. It is equally intriguing that a January/February 2017 article in *Foreign Affairs* was titled "World Order 2.0: The Case for Sovereign Obligation." The author of the article, Richard Haass president of the CFR, writes, "*An approach to international order premised solely on respect for sovereignty, together with the maintenance of the balance of power necessary to secure it, is no longer sufficient. The globe's traditional operating system—call it World Order 1.0—has been built around the protection and prerogatives of states. It is increasingly inadequate in today's globalized world. Little now stays local; just about anyone and anything, from tourists, terrorists, and refugees to e-mails, diseases, dollars, and greenhouse gases, can reach almost anywhere. The result is that what goes on inside a country can no longer be considered the concern of that country alone. Today's circumstances call for an updated operating system—call it World Order 2.0—that includes not only the rights of sovereign states but also those states' obligations to others.*" This short paragraph sounds very much like a call for a one-world-government; which, of course, would be controlled by the banks.

Secret Roundtable: Bilderberg

The Council on Foreign Nations is not the only roundtable created by the wealthy. The Bilderberg

Group, a group of 120 to 150 of political, corporate, finance, and academic elites from Europe and North America, was founded in 1954 by David Rockefeller. They meet annually for a three-day conference to promote dialogue between Europe and North America on a variety of issues from monetary policy, environmental challenges to the promotion international security. Sounds harmless and helpful, right? In 2007 Daniel Estulin, an investigative journalist, published his bestselling book *The True Story of the Bilderberg Group.* Estulin describes the group as follows. *"These people want an empire. The idea behind each and every Bilderberg meeting is to create what they themselves call the aristocracy of purpose between European and North American elites on the best way to manage the planet. In other words, the creation of a global network of giant cartels, more powerful than any nation on earth, destined to control the necessities of life of the rest of humanity, obviously from their vantage point, for our own good and in our benefit, the great unwashed as they call us. They are destroying the world economy on purpose."* Scary stuff, yet it fits a pattern of wealthy elites vying for control of money and power.

Secret Roundtable: Trilateral Commission

There is still one more roundtable to consider, the Trilateral Commission (TLC). The TLC was created in

1973 by President Jimmy Carter's future national security advisor Zbigniew Brezinski and David Rockefeller. (Membership is by invitation only.) Their original stated mission of TLC was, *"When the first triennium of the Trilateral Commission was launched in 1973, the most immediate purpose was to draw together the highest-level unofficial group possible to look together at the key common problems facing our three areas. At a deeper level, there was a sense that the United States was no longer in such a singular leadership position as it had been in earlier post-World War II years, and that a more shared form of leadership—including Europe and Japan in particular—would be needed for the international system to navigate successfully the major challenges of the coming years."*[51] This sounds very similar to the goals of CFR and the Bilderberg Group. Senator Barry Goldwater had even stronger feelings about TLC. In his 1979 book *With No Apologies* Goldwater wrote, *"The Trilateral Commission is international and is intended to be the vehicle for multinational consolidation of the commercial and banking interests by seizing control of the political government of the United States. The TLC represents a skillful, coordinated effort to seize control and consolidate the four centers of power – political, monetary, intellectual and ecclesiastical."*

How Roundtables Influence

As we shall learn, America's foreign policies since the creation of the first roundtable, CFR, have failed to help the citizens of the United States. So how do these roundtable groups influence government policy? As we have learned, they are appointed to cabinet positions in the White House. Let's take a closer look at the underbelly of roundtable influence. We begin this examination with the election of Woodrow Wilson ten years prior to the creation of the Council on Foreign Relations.

Wilson's election to the presidency was a significant first step in the creation of the CFR. Wilson's top advisor was Colonel Edward M. House, a wealthy cotton plantation owner, and banking investor, was a founding member of the CFR. House nurtured connections with many Wall Street bankers and business elites of his time and shared their ideas on who should control a nation's currency. As a consummate negotiator, House spearheaded the Federal Reserve Act through Congress while convincing Wilson to sign the new act into law. Remember, although the word federal appears in the title, the Federal Reserve is privately owned by member banks and is not subject to oversight by Congress or the President. The Fed, with its owner banks, makes its own policies, is the overseer and supplier of reserves, and grants member banks access to public funds.

Wilson was a smart man and knew of the founding fathers' warnings about the creation of a private central bank. For example, Thomas Jefferson wrote, *"If the American people ever allow private banks to control the issue of their currency, first by inflation, then by deflation, the banks...will deprive the people of all property until their children wake-up homeless on the continent their fathers conquered... The issuing power should be taken from the banks and restored to the people, to whom it properly belongs."*[52] James Madison echoed, *"History records that the money changers have used every form of abuse, intrigue, deceit, and violent means possible to maintain their control over governments by controlling money and its issuance."*[53] After the creation of the Fed others have expressed opinions similar to the founding fathers. Congressman Louis McFadden, Chairman of the House Committee on Banking and Currency from 1920-31, stated, *"When the Federal Reserve Act was passed, the people of these United States did not perceive that a world banking system was being set up here. A super-state controlled by international bankers and industrialists...acting together to enslave the world...Every effort has been made by the Fed to conceal its powers but the truth is—the Fed has usurped the government."*[54] The argument the founding fathers' made and was ignored is this: in order to effectively control a government all that is needed is to gain control over the nation's money.

The Truman Doctrine

From Wilson, we move on to foreign affair disasters of President Harry S. Truman. Six high-level advisors of his administration were members of the CFR. They included secretary of state, secretary of defense, Marshall Plan administrator, high commissioner to Germany, and two state department consultants. Although Truman is credited with ending World War II via the atomic bomb, he also created a foreign policy disaster commonly known as the Truman Doctrine. The original intent of the Doctrine was to provide free financial aid and military support to Greece and Turkey to fend off communist takeovers of their governments. Unfortunately, the Truman Doctrine extended far beyond Greece and Turkey. It laid the groundwork for the Marshall Plan designed by CFR member and advisor to Truman, George F. Kennan. The Plan gave European nations $13 billion to rebuild economies and facilitate global trade and open markets to the United States. The Marshall Plan gave Washington some control and influence over the Europeans as free money always comes with strings attached. Thomas Wilson, Marshall Plan Information Officer to England and France, 1947-1952 had this to say about the Marshall Plan, "*I thought like most of us, there would be a United States of Europe within a decade.*"55 Added William Parks, Greek-Turkish Aid Program for the Marshall Plan Administration, 1948-1955, "*With the enactment of the E.C. Act [Economic Cooperation Act] in April of 1948, to the surprise of many people, including, I suspect, the planners in the Department of State, the Congress, in approving this $20 billion, four-year program, which was the conceptual framework of the Marshall Plan, decided that under no circumstances would it entrust this highly operational program to the Department of State. It insisted upon the creation of an independent agency, to be called the Economic Cooperation Administration (ECA), to assume this awesome responsibility. Beyond that, the President determined that the program should be headed by an outstanding, prestigious U.S. citizen with a proven track record in business and management. He selected the late Paul Hoffman for this purpose.*56 As it happens, in 1935 Hoffman was installed as president of Studebaker Corporation by Goldman Sachs and Company. The Marshall Plan came with many conditions that certainly fit within the CFR's goal of creating one world order.

The Marshall Plan was only the beginning of a never-ending policy of interfering with independent nations and their disputes with other foreign governments. It was the beginning of America as the international police officer. Truman's belief that the United States should support free nations who are resisting attempted suppression by outside pressures led to the United States involvement in Korean back in 1950. Up until WWII, the Korean peninsula was governed by Japan. Just as the Allies split Germany in half, in 1945 Korea was divided into two sections. North Korea was awarded to Russia and South Korea was occupied by the United States. Both the North and South quickly developed independent governments. North Korea took a communist form while South Korea accepted an anti-communism dictator. Truman's new secretary of state and former undersecretary of the U.S. Department of Defense, Dean Acheson was a member of the CFR and had helped shape the Truman Doctrine, promoted the formation of the North Atlantic Treaty Organization (NATO), and helped frame the Cold War between the United States and Russia. When North Korean troops crossed the border separating the two Koreas in June 1950, Acheson advised Truman to send U.S. soldiers to South Korea to protect the South from communism. To CFR members, the only thing preventing a new world order was communism – which had the same goal. Commenting on the title of his autobiography, Acheson said *Present at the Creation* was chosen to represent, *"the building by America of a new world, out of the wartime rubble of the old—or, at any rate, of half a new world, the free half, while an ally turned enemy, the Soviet Union, built the other half.*"[57]

Vietnam and Communism

After the Korean conflict, came the Vietnam War. Actually, America's involvement in Vietnam preceded military action in North Korea. On May 8, 1950, two months before America's involvement in Korea, U.S. Secretary of State Acheson proclaimed that, *"The United States Government convinced that neither national independence nor democratic evolution exist in any area dominated by Soviet imperialism considers the situation to be such as to warrant its according economic aid and military equipment to the Associated States of Indochina and to France in order to assist them in restoring stability and permitting these states to pursue their peaceful and democratic development."*[58] And on May 11, 1950, Assistant Secretary of State Dean Rusk, also a member of CFR, made the following statement. *"A special survey mission, headed by R. Allen Griffin, has just returned from Southeast Asia and reported on economic and technical assistance needed in that area. Its overall recommendations for the area are modest and total in the neighborhood of $60 million. The Department is working on plans to implement that program at once. Secretary Acheson on Monday in Paris cited the urgency of the situation applying in the associate* *states of Viet-Nam, Laos, and Cambodia. The Department is working jointly with ECA to implement the economic and technical assistance recommendations for Indochina as well as the other states of Southeast Asia and anticipates that this program will get underway in the immediate future. Military assistance for Southeast Asia is being worked out by the Department of Defense in cooperation with the Department of State, and the details will not be made public for security reasons. Military assistance needs will be made from the President's emergency fund of $75 million provided under MDAP for the general area of China. Economic assistance needs will be met from the ECA China Aid funds, part of which both Houses of Congress have indicated will be made available for the general area of China. Final legislative action is still pending on this authorization but is expected to be completed within the next week."*[59] Between 1950 and 1954, the United States funded the French's war effort in Vietnam to the tune of 78 percent of all costs.[60]

The United States interests in Vietnam were not altruistic. We didn't care who governed Vietnam, as long as it wasn't the communists. Southeast Asia was a large untapped market just waiting to become trade partners with the United States. Communism threatened the opening of Southeastern Asia markets. In 1950, Vietnam was still under control of

France. However, Russia knew that the Vietnamese wanted self-governance and they backed Ho Chi Minh, a revolutionary leader and president of the newly formed Democratic Republic of Vietnam (North Vietnam) from 1945 to 1969. Several times during Ho Chi Minh's career he had petitioned the United States to recognize Vietnam's independence and support the end of the French colony status. The first time was to Woodrow Wilson in 1919. Wilson refused to meet with him. The second opportunity came in 1945 when he requested Truman to recognize an independent Vietnam under the Atlantic Charter. Truman did not respond. These were missed opportunities by the United States to influence the future of Vietnam. Then, in 1950, the Soviet Union's General Secretary Joseph Stalin recognized the Democratic Republic of Vietnam as a nation. Ho Chi Minh now had access to war supplies and in 1954 defeated the French. A peace treaty, the Geneva Accords, separated Vietnam into two sections. The North governed by Ho Chi Minh, and the South governed by the State of South Vietnam.

After the Geneva Accords were signed Secretary of State John Foster Dulles, a CFR member, developed the Southeast Asian Treaty Organization (SEATO) to join the different former colonies of Southeast Asia into one cohesive unit free of communist rule. Only two southeastern nations signed on, the Philippines and Thailand. SEATO was basically a failure as it served no real purpose except for one. Dulles used the SEATO charter as a rationale for American involvement in Vietnam. (Dulles included Vietnam in the SEATO charter even though neither the North nor South signed the agreement.) Elections were scheduled to take place in 1956 to unify Vietnam, but the United States refused to allow the election to take place. Dulles was afraid that communists might win the election making the unified country a communist nation. As a result, Vietnam stayed separated at the 17th parallel. The lack of elections set the stage for further conflict between the North and South.

CFR Lies Push U.S. to War in Southeast Asia

Presidents' Eisenhower and Kennedy placed military advisors in South Vietnam to assist with training of South Vietnamese soldiers. But the real fighting with U.S troops began with President Lyndon Johnson. Although Johnson was not a member of the CFR, his Secretaries of State and Defense, as well as the Under Secretary of State, were. In early August 1964, Johnson told Congress that North Vietnamese patrol boats had fired upon the U.S. Destroyer Maddox in international waters. He reported that the Maddox came under fire again two days later. Both times the Maddox returned fire. As a result of Johnson's testimony, Congress passed the Gulf of Tonkin Resolution which allowed the president to take any necessary steps, including the use of force to help any SEATO member requiring help in defending its freedom. In effect, the resolution gave the president war-making powers without a Congressional declaration of war. As it turns out, Johnson lied to Congress or Johnson was lied to by Secretary of State McNamara or both. The Maddox was not in international waters. It and other destroyers were in North Vietnam's territorial waters with the intent of provoking North Vietnam to attack while they gathered intelligence on their radar systems. U.S. ships fired on the North Vietnamese ships first. The following text comes directly from the Pentagon Papers released by the federal government in 1971.

"Unknown to more than a limited number of Government officials were a variety of covert military or quasi-military operations being conducted at the expense of North Vietnam. U.S. naval forces had undertaken intermittent patrol operations in the Gulf of Tonkin designed to acquire visual, electronic and photographic intelligence on infiltration activities and coastal navigation from North Vietnam to the South. To carry out these missions, destroyers were assigned to tracks between fixed points and according to stipulated schedules. Designated DESOTO Patrols, the first such operation of 1964 occurred during the period 28 February- 10 March. On this patrol the U.S.S.

Craig was authorized to approach to within 4 n .m. of the North Vietnamese mainland, 15 n.m. of the Chinese mainland and 12 n.m. of Chinese-held islands. No incidents were reported as resulting from this action. The next DESOTO Patrol did not occur until 31 July on which the U.S.S. Maddox was restricted to a track not closer than 8 n.m. off the North Vietnamese mainland. Its primary mission assigned on 17 July was to determine DRV coastal activity along the full extent of the patrol track. Other specific intelligence requirements were assigned as follows:

a) *Location and identification of all radar transmitters and estimate of range capabilities*

b) *Navigational and hydro information along the routes traversed and particular navigational lights characteristics, landmarks, buoys, currents and tidal information, river mouths and channel accessibility*

c) *Monitoring a junk force with density of surface traffic pattern*

d) *Sampling electronic environment radars and navigation aids*

e) *Photography of opportunities in support of above... "*

"Separate coastal patrol operations were being conducted by South Vietnamese naval forces. These were designed to uncover and interdict efforts to smuggle personnel and supplies into the South in support of the VC insurgency. This operation had first been organized with U.S. assistance in December 1961 to support it a fleet of motorized junks was built, partially financed with U.S. military assistance funds. During 1964 these vessels operated almost continually in attempts to intercept communist seaborne logistical operations. As Secretary McNamara told Senate committees, 'In the first seven months of this year (1964), they have searched 149,000 junks, some 570,000 people. This is a tremendous operation endeavoring to close the seacoasts of over 900 miles. In the process of that action, as the junk patrol has increased in strength they have moved farther and farther north endeavoring to find the source of the infiltration.'"

"In addition to these acknowledged activities; the GVN was also conducting a number of operations against North Vietnam to which it did not publicly admit. Covert operations were carried out by South Vietnamese or hired personnel and supported by U.S. training and logistical efforts. Outlined within OPLAN 34A, these operations had been underway theoretically since February but had experienced what the JCS called a slow beginning. Despite an ultimate objective of helping convince the North

Vietnamese leadership that it is in its own self-interest to desist from its aggressive policies, few operations designed to harass the enemy were carried out successfully during the February-May period. Nevertheless, citing DRV reactions tending to substantiate the premise that Hanoi is expending substantial resources in defensive measures, the JCS concluded that the potential of the OPLAN 34A program remained high and urged its continuation through Phase II (June-September)."

"Operations including air-infiltration of sabotage teams, underwater demolition and seizures of communist junks were approved for the period, and a few were carried by specially trained GVN forces during June and July."

"In addition to both the open and covert operations already underway, a number of other actions intended to bring pressure against North Vietnam had been recommended to the White House. Receiving considerable attention among Administration officials during May and June was a proposed request for a Congressional Resolution, reaffirming support by the legislators for Presidential action to resist Communist advances in Southeast Asia during an election year. In some respects paralleling this domestic initiative, the President was urged to present to the United Nations the detailed case assembled by the

Government supporting the charges of DRV aggression against South Vietnam and Laos. He was also urged to authorize periodic deployments of additional forces toward Southeast Asia as a means of demonstrating U.S. resolve to undertake whatever measures were required to resist aggression in that region. Moreover, in OPLAN 37-64, there was fully developed a listing of forces to be deployed as a deterrent to communist escalation in reaction to U.S. /GVN actions against North Vietnam. Finally, it was recommended that the President make the decision to use selected and carefully graduated military force against North Vietnam if necessary to improve non-Communist prospects in South Vietnam and Laos."

OPLAN 34A as mentioned in the Pentagon Papers was implemented on July 30, 1964, three days prior to the first Maddox incident, and refers to a plan approved by Johnson authorizing the shelling of two North Vietnamese islands in the Gulf of Tonkin. OPLAN 34 was designed to provoke the North Vietnamese into a confrontation with the U.S. Navy. So essentially, the United States Congress passed the Gulf of Tonkin Resolution based on false and deceitful information given to them by the Johnson Administration. The National Security Agency (NSA) eventually took the blame saying they mishandled intelligence and admitted there was no second attack on the Maddox.[61] U.S. military ground and air involvement in Vietnam seems to have been based on untruths.

Interestingly enough, Richard Helms, director of the CIA and a member of CFR, controlled this operation and not the Navy. But then again, if the aim of the CFR was to minimize communism to create a one nation world, driving the communist regime from North Vietnam could only be accomplished through war. There is more evidence that the CFR had influenced the Vietnam War decision. After the Gulf of Tonkin lies, later in August 1964, U.S. Ambassador to South Vietnam and a CFR member, Maxwell Taylor recommended a well-thought out and organized bombing attack on North Vietnam to begin on January 1, 1965.[62] Why was this significant? Johnson was running for re-election in 1964 on a peace campaign. He had repeatedly told the American people he did not seek war in Vietnam. A January 1, 1965, target was a post-election date and assumed that Johnson would be re-elected to the presidency. In September of 1964, John McNaughton Assistant Secretary for International Security Affairs and a member of CFR urged the president to undertake covert actions in North Vietnam and Laos to provoke a North Vietnam response giving Johnson a reason to escalate the war. McNaughton advised Johnson to wait until after the election to put the plans in action.[63] Meanwhile, as late as October 21, 1964, Johnson gave a speech at Akron University in which he said, "We are not about to send American boys 9 or 10,000 miles away from home to do what Asian boys ought to be doing for themselves."[64]

Once elected, Johnson wasted no time in escalating the war. And he did so with the backing of the CFR. *"In addition to the CFR members that held official positions in the Johnson Administration, its leaders organized a 48-person Committee for an Effective and Durable Peace in Asia to support the war effort. The committee ran an ad in the New York Times and 13 other newspapers across the country in early September 1965, which expressed its agreement with Johnson's war aims in a ten-point statement of principles. It stressed that he acted rightly and in the national interest in sending American troops into Vietnam. A Wall Street lawyer, Arthur H. Dean, the country's chief negotiator at the talks that ended the fighting in Korea, chaired the committee. Most of the 48 members were bankers, corporate lawyers, and college presidents from all parts of the country, but there were several corporate CEOs as well"*[65] (Arthur Dean was also a member of the Bilderberg Group.) It seems fairly clear that Johnson was controlled by the CFR.

Richard Nixon who was elected president in 1968 was a former member of the CFR having resigned in 1962. However, that did not stop him from appointing over 100 CFR members to his cabinet. And the Vietnam War continued, but not without help from Nixon during the 1968 presidential cycle. The New York Times reported that in October 1968, Herbert Humphrey (a Democratic like Johnson) was closing in on Nixon's lead. Henry Kissinger, a CFR member and future Secretary of State contacted Nixon, "*that a deal was in the works: If Johnson would halt all bombing of North Vietnam, the Soviets pledged to have Hanoi engage in constructive talks to end a war that had already claimed 30,000 American lives.*"[66] Nixon got word to the president of South Vietnam that Johnson was not to be trusted and to delay peace talks until after the U.S. election. Nixon had a good reason for interfering, for if peace talks had taken place and the war with Vietnam ended, Humphrey would surely have won the election ending Nixon's political career. Kissinger also had a reason to manipulate Nixon into taking action. Kissinger has been perhaps the most vocal CFR member calling for a new world order. In his 2014 book *World Order*, Kissinger argues nations wrongly define their own concepts of order with each considering itself the center of the world. He believes we must pursue a concept of world order – a global architecture controlled by a few elite members of society.

Reagan Enable Roundtables

During the 1980 presidential campaign, candidate Ronald Reagan openly criticized President Jimmy Carter and the nineteen staffers of his administration for being members of the Trilateral Commission. In fact, he pledged to have the group investigated if he was elected. Reagan did not like the Trilateral and pledged not to select any TLC members to his administration. A funny thing happened at the Republican National Convention in which Reagan was nominated to run for president. Many thought Reagan would select former President Gerald Ford as his running mate and vice-president. Reagan wanted Ford as VP, but during the convention, Ford declined Reagan's offer. With only one day separating Reagan from nomination he reluctantly nominated George H.W. Bush as vice president. This was an interesting choice because Reagan did not like Bush and Bush did not like Reagan. Bush was also a member of the Trilateral Commission and the CFR and had previously stated he would not accept the role of VP. *"Reagan rolled on toward the nomination thereafter—leading reporters to pepper the still-campaigning Bush with questions about his availability for the vice-presidential nomination. With his back up, Bush scornfully dismissed the possibility, invoking the famous disavowal of Civil War General William Tecumseh Sherman in 1884 that 'I will not accept if nominated, and will not serve if elected.' Bush shortened and strengthened his own rejection to a pithy 'Take Sherman and cubed it,' as he continued in the primaries in his failed effort to overtake Reagan."*[67]

Once elected, Reagan changed his position on the Roundtables as his transition team consisted of 10 from TLC, 10 Bilderberg members, and 28 from the CFR. Reagan's three top cabinet appointees were members of the CFR: Secretary of State Alexander Haig, Secretary of Defense Casper Weinberger, and Secretary of the Treasury Donald Regan.

Without trying to sound like a conspiracy theorist, it is interesting to note that two months after Reagan's inauguration, an attempt on his life was made by would-be assassin John W. Hinckley, Jr. Reagan was shot in the chest but recovered. What is so special about the event is the assassin's father, John, Sr was a wealthy oilman and longtime friend of Vice President Bush. On the day of the shooting, Hinckley Sr received notice from the Department of Energy stating *"The government might be forced to penalize the family business to the tune of $2 million."*[68] The day after the shooting the notice was withdrawn. Had Reagan died, Bush would have become president. Hinckley Jr. was found not guilty by reason of insanity.

CFR, TLC, Support Al Qaeda, and Terrorism

Beginning in the late 1970's the CIA, led by CFR directors, began funding and sending arms to the mujahedeen Islamic militants who were fighting to drive the Soviets out of Afghanistan. One of the mujahideen fighters was a wealthy son of a Saudi businessman named Osama Bin Laden. Zbigniew Brzezinski, National Security Advisor under President Carter, traveled to Afghanistan in 1979 and met Bin Laden. He told Bin Laden their cause was right, God was on their side, and to make the Russians bleed for as long as they can.[69] An article in the *Foreign Policy Journal* also supports the argument that the U.S. government created al Qaeda. *"With America's massive and indispensable military backing in the 1980s, Afghanistan's last secular government (bringing women into the 20th century) was overthrown, and out of the victorious Mujahedeen arose al Qaeda. During this same period, the United States was supporting the infamous Khmer Rouge of Cambodia; yes, the same charming lads of Pol Pot and The Killing Fields. President Carter's National Security Adviser, Zbigniew Brzezinski, was a leading force behind the US support of both the Mujahedeen and the Khmer Rouge."*[70] When the Russians were defeated in 1988, Bin Laden formed al Qaeda and declared a holy war against the United States and other non-Islamic governments. Thanks to Brzezinski and the CIA, Bin

Laden had money, arms, training, and the experience necessary to carry out worldwide terrorist attacks. The supporting of Bin Laden and the Mujahedeen in Afghanistan should be considered one of America's biggest foreign policy mistakes.

But there is more to the Afghan-Russian war then the creation of al Qaeda. Just as the United States provoked North Vietnam into battle, President Carter, under Brzezinski's urging, provoked the Soviet Union into invading Afghanistan in 1980. The following is an interview with Brzezinski conducted in 1998 by a French magazine *Le Nouvel Observateur*.[71]

"***Question***: *The former director of the CIA, Robert Gates, stated in his memoirs that the American intelligence services began to aid the Mujahidin in Afghanistan six months before the Soviet intervention. Is this period, you were the national security advisor to President Carter. You therefore played a key role in this affair. Is this correct?*"

"***Brzezinski***: *Yes. According to the official version of history, CIA aid to the Mujahidin began during 1980, that is to say, after the Soviet army invaded Afghanistan on December 24, 1979. But the reality, closely guarded until now, is completely otherwise: Indeed, it was July 3, 1979, that President Carter signed the first directive for secret aid to the* *opponents of the pro-Soviet regime in Kabul. And that very day, I wrote a note to the president in which I explained to him that in my opinion this aid was going to induce a Soviet military intervention [emphasis added throughout]."*

*"**Q**: Despite this risk, you were an advocate of this covert action. But perhaps you yourself desired this Soviet entry into the war and looked for a way to provoke it?"*

*"**B**: It wasn't quite like that. We didn't push the Russians to intervene, but we knowingly increased the probability that they would."*

*"**Q**: When the Soviets justified their intervention by asserting that they intended to fight against secret US involvement in Afghanistan, nobody believed them. However, there was an element of truth in this. You don't regret any of this today?"*

*"**B**: Regret what? That secret operation was an excellent idea. It had the effect of drawing the Russians into the Afghan trap and you want me to regret it? The day that the Soviets officially crossed the border, I wrote to President Carter, essentially: 'We now have the opportunity of giving to the USSR its Vietnam War.' Indeed, for almost 10 years, Moscow had to carry on a war that was unsustainable for the regime, a conflict that bought*

about the demoralization and finally the breakup of the Soviet empire."

*"**Q**: And neither do you regret having supported Islamic fundamentalism, which has given arms and advice to future terrorists?"*

*"**B**: What is more important in world history? The Taliban or the collapse of the Soviet empire? Some agitated Muslims or the liberation of Central Europe and the end of the cold war?"*

*"**Q**: "Some agitated Muslims"? But it has been said and repeated: Islamic fundamentalism represents a world menace today..."*

*"**B**: Nonsense! It is said that the West has a global policy in regard to Islam. That is stupid: There isn't a global Islam. Look at Islam in a rational manner, without demagoguery or emotionalism. It is the leading religion of the world with 1.5 billion followers. But what is there in common among fundamentalist Saudi Arabia, moderate Morocco, militarist Pakistan, pro-Western Egypt, or secularist Central Asia? Nothing more than what unites the Christian countries..."*

Compare Brzezinski's 1998 statement about Muslim violence with an August 2016 comment on the same subject.[72] *"The fifth verity is that the currently violent political awakening among post-*

colonial Muslims is, in part, a belated reaction to their occasionally brutal suppression mostly by European powers. It fuses a delayed but deeply felt sense of injustice with a religious motivation that is unifying large numbers of Muslims against the outside world."

It seems that same Muslims used as bait by Brzezinski are now a global threat. And with good reason. Remember the 2011 Arab Spring, a movement by citizens in many the Middle East and Northern African countries demonstrating for democracy and an end to oppressive governments. Brzezinski saw an opportunity to meddle once again in the Middle East by advocating the overthrow Libya's President Muammar Gaddafi through NATO. Brzezinski was not the only one pressuring President Obama to vote yes on the UN Council Resolution 1973 authorizing military intervention in Libya. Secretary of State Hillary Clinton also pressured the president. (It should come as no surprise that Mrs. Clinton's husband former President Bill Clinton is also a member of the Trilateral.) The resolution was approved, and the United States led the assault on Libya, mainly by bombing Gaddafi's headquarters and palaces. Seven months later Gaddafi died and a permanent instability in the Middle East born.

As it turns out, the overthrowing of Gaddafi had nothing to do with democracy. It was about gold.

Gaddafi was planning to establish a gold-backed African currency tied to the Libyan dinar. Gaddafi reportedly had stockpiled over a 143 tons of gold, and a similar amount in silver.[73] His plan was to sell Libyan oil (Libya was the largest African oil producer) only in dinars. U.S. dollars would no longer be accepted. If you are Brzezinski advocating for a global economy or an elite controlling a central bank, Gaddafi's plan to control the economies of the African continent was a death blow. And death came, but not to the western central banking domain but to Gaddafi. Five years later Libya remains in a state of turmoil and chaos. Thousands of civilians have been killed, and roughly 500,000 Libyans are now homeless. There are about 2,000 different militia groups in Libya, including ISIS and al Qaeda.

We must further consider Zbigniew Brzezinski and his role in the American foreign policy. Brzezinski had been an advisor to John F, Kennedy, Lyndon B. Johnson, Hubert Humphrey, Jimmy Carter, George H.W. Bush, and Barack Obama. That's fifty years of influencing powerful politicians. To better understand Brzezinski's worldview philosophy we need to look no farther than his 1971 book entitled, *Between Two Ages: America's Role in the Technetronic Era.* In it he wrote, *"The nation-state as a fundamental unit of man's organized life has ceased to be the principal creative force: International banks and multinational corporations are acting and planning in terms that are far in advance of the political concepts of the nation-state."*[74] This was Brzezinski's way of saying a new global political order was needed to control the world's economy. In other words, non-governmental institutions (the wealthy elite) should control the global economy. Governments then become political subordinates of economic power.

Iraqi Wars

The wars in Iraq, although different in scope and context from Korea and Vietnam, were nevertheless, the result of roundtable influences. In August 1990 Saddam Hussein, ruler of Iraq, invaded neighboring Kuwait. The United States organized an international coalition of soldiers to battle Hussein's forces in Kuwait. The American-led forces quickly forced Hussein back across the border. Then something unusual happened. The coalition forces stopped pursuing Hussein's army. Normally when an invading army is repelled, the conquering militia captures the attacker's capital and removes the sitting government. President George H.W. Bush, a member of both the CFR and the Trilateral and his National Security Advisor Brent Scowcroft felt going into Baghdad exceeded the United Nations' mandate. (Bush's Secretary of Defense Dick Cheney was also a member of CFR and TLC.) In 1998 Bush and Scowcroft wrote, *"While we hoped that a popular revolt or coup would topple Saddam, neither the United States nor the countries of the region wished to see the breakup of the Iraqi state. We were concerned about the long-term balance of power at the head of the Gulf. Breaking up the Iraqi state would pose its own destabilizing problems. Trying to eliminate Saddam, extending the ground war into an occupation of Iraq, would have violated our guideline about not changing objectives in midstream, engaging in "mission creep," and would have incurred incalculable human and political costs."*[75]

The fear shared by Bush, Scowcroft, and Cheney was that a conquered Iraq could easily be subdivided into territorial possessions of other Russian friendly nations such as Iran, Syria, or even Turkey. This explanation is in keeping with the CFR and Trilateral philosophy of containing Russia and developing an anti-communist global economy.

Yet, despite that fear, President George W. Bush, son of George H.W. Bush, and his Vice President Dick Cheney invaded Iraq in 2003 for reasons not fully known. The Bush 43 administration contained many Bush 41 staffers who may have felt that Iraq was unfinished business. Staffers and CFR members who served both Bush administrations include:

- Cheney

- National Security Advisor, Condoleezza Rice
- Chairman of the Foreign Intelligence Advisory Board, Brent Scowcroft
- Deputy National Security Advisor, Stephen Hadley
- Chief of Staff for the Vice President, L. Lewis Libby
- Assistant Secretary of Defense, Paul Wolfowitz

We now know that President Bush wanted Saddam Hussein out of power long before the September 11, 2001, attacks on New York and Washington. During his presidential campaign, Bush mentioned on more than one occasion that Hussein was a threat to the United States. During a *60 Minutes* interview with Leslie Stahl, former Treasury Secretary under Bush 43 Paul O'Neill said, "*From the very beginning, there was a conviction, that Saddam Hussein was a bad person and that he needed to go...going after Saddam was topic 'A' 10 days after the inauguration, eight months before Sept. 11.*"[76]

More evidence that the Bush Administration had decided to oust Hussein prior to the September 11, 2001, attacks is provided by the National Security Archive Electronic Briefing Book No. 326 of declassified documents. The following passage details what took place in the White House prior to September 11, 2001.[77]

"When the new administration's principals (agency heads) met for the first time at the end of January (2001) it was to discuss the Middle East, including Bush's planned disengagement from efforts to resolve the Arab-Israeli conflict, and the issue of 'How Iraq is destabilizing the region.' Bush directed the Pentagon to look into military options for Iraq and the CIA to improve intelligence on the country. At a February 1 principals meeting Paul Wolfowitz lobbied for arming the Iraqi opposition. When the deputies (agency seconds-in-command) committee met in April for its first discussion of terrorism since the president took office and counterterrorism chief Richard Clarke attempted to focus on Osama bin Laden and the Taliban – five months before 9/11 -- Wolfowitz tried to change the subject to Iraq."

"At around this time, the U.S. learned that Iraq was interested in buying 60,000 aluminum tubes (advertisements appeared on the internet). A CIA analyst who was not a nuclear weapons specialist became convinced that the high-strength alloy tubes could only be intended for uranium enrichment centrifuges to manufacture nuclear weapons. The CIA (led by George Tenet a CFR member) endorsed his opinion and passed it on to Bush in a President's

Daily Brief. An April 10 follow-up report was circulated among national security officials and the CIA analysis was immediately questioned by nuclear weapons experts. On April 11 scientists led by the chief of the Oak Ridge National Laboratory's Advanced Technology Division reported that the diameter of the tubes was off by 50 percent (compared to a centrifuge that Iraq tested in 1990), among other discrepancies. The Oak Ridge team concluded the tubes were probably not intended for centrifuges."

"On May 9 the Energy Department reported in a Daily Intelligence Highlight, published on a website used by the White House and the intelligence community that the intercepted tubes were quite similar to ones that Iraq used to build conventional rocket launchers. In June the U.S. got direct access to the intercepted shipment. The CIA analyst admitted they were the wrong size for standard centrifuges, but said they matched the dimensions of those used for a centrifuge designed in the 1950s by a German scientist. The scientist told him they weren't even close."

"On July 13, 2001, the deputies committee met to discuss Iraq and Wolfowitz said again that to achieve "regime change" the U.S. should provide more support for Iraqi opposition groups, recognize a provisional government, and create an enclave in

the south that would be called 'Free Iraq.' The U.S. would then give 'Free Iraq' frozen Iraqi assets. The protected zone would be expanded to expropriate Iraq's oil fields and their revenues."

"In a July 27 memo to Rice, Rumsfeld outlined a range of policy options and said definitively, 'Within a few years the U.S. will undoubtedly have to confront a Saddam armed with nuclear weapons.' He concluded, 'If Saddam's regime were ousted, we would have a much-improved position in the region and elsewhere,' and, 'a major success in Iraq would enhance U.S. credibility and influence throughout the region.'"

"On August 1 the deputies gave a top secret paper on Iraq to the principals with the title of 'A Liberation Strategy', discussing CIA and other U.S. support for Iraqi opposition groups and possible direct U.S. military action. Wolfowitz said his enclave strategy would easily succeed."

Barack Obama promised to bring change to Washington. He didn't. His cabinet was filled with TLC members. They included:

- Secretary of Treasury, Tim Geithner
- Ambassador to the United Nations, Susan Rice; National Security Advisor
- National Security Advisor, Gen. James L. Jones

- Deputy National Security Advisor, Thomas Donilon
- Chairman, Economic Recovery Committee, Paul Volker
- Director of National Intelligence, Admiral Dennis C. Blair
- Assistant Secretary of State, Asia & Pacific, Kurt M. Campbell
- Deputy Secretary of State, James Steinberg
- State Department, Special Envoy, Richard Haass – now president of CFR
- State Department, Special Envoy, Dennis Ross
- State Department, Special Envoy, Richard Holbrooke
- Brent Scowcroft has served as an unofficial advisor to Obama and was mentor to Defense Secretary Robert Gates
- Zbigniew Brzezinski served as Obama's foreign policy advisor during his 2008 presidential campaign and continued to serve unofficially as an advisor through 2012.

This group of roundtable members were appointed to highly important positions that control the areas of finance, national security, and foreign policy. That was not change. That was taking the government down the same path as traveled for the past 100 years. This group of elites failed miserably. Take Secretary of Treasury Geithner for example.

Geithner came to Treasury from the Fed, where he was president of the Federal Reserve Bank of New York. This despite the fact that he failed to pay his full share of federal income taxes from the years 2001 through 2004. He claimed it was an honest mistake. Maybe it was, but should someone who fails to pay his taxes be appointed to the federal agency that controls the collection of taxes? Was it a mistake when Geithner negotiated the deal that allowed the Italian car manufacturer Fiat to purchase Chrysler and save them from bankruptcy? It just happens that Luca di Montezemolo, a member of the Trilateral, was chairman of Fiat's board of directors at the time the deal was closed. Was Geithner saving Chrysler or helping to create one global economy controlled by the elites? I guess it depends on your perspective. Do you believe in capitalism and the free markets? Or do you believe in a one-world economy controlled by a small group of elites?

Summary

After nearly 45 years of TLC and 100 years of CFR meddling in world affairs and controlling U.S foreign policy, the United States is in a much weaker position as an influencer and leader of world issues. U.S. relations with long-time friends have begun to unravel, Russia is exerting increased power in Eastern Europe, and even in the Middle East. And more and more citizens of other nations have

169

developed a hatred of the United States. And why shouldn't they? Look what we have done to Iraq, Libya, Syria, Somalia, Afghanistan, and others. Our number one and two foreign policy tools are war and sanctions. Both bring pain and suffering to citizens rather than governments. And they rarely bring about the policy changes sought. The Roundtables want a one-world economy and culture, but everything they have done has had the opposite effect. Rather than establishing peace and world security, the Roundtable decisions have served as nothing more than incubators for global terrorism. And Russia, Iran, and North Korea have all been emboldened by the United States continued a string of miscalculations and failed policies.

Meanwhile, China has grown into the world's largest trading partner among developing nations. Over the past twenty years, while the United States has relied on warfare as its main diplomatic tool, China has been busy investing huge sums of money in the US, the UK, Australia, Japan, Brazil, Russia, and Africa. China is using capitalism to build strong international relationships and to change geopolitical thinking. The U.S. foreign policy of sanctions, isolation, and military actions has only produced hatred and distrust of the U.S.

How Do We Get Control

There are no easy fixes for this one. Small elite membership organizations are not illegal, nor should they be. Nor is there anything wrong with an ideology that believes a united world would mean an end, or least a reduction, of violence and wars and an increase in worldwide prosperity. The challenge is that some members of these roundtables believe that only a small group of elites have the wisdom and knowledge to manage the affairs of the world. They know best. They get to dole out the sour-tasting medicine we must take for our own good. Or so they think. They are wrong. People have beliefs, dreams, emotions, fears, prejudices, and biases. Humans can be controlled and manipulated to a point. But we all want and will fight for the freedom to control our own destiny. A one-world government cannot duplicate the benefits and liberties offered through local control. But that's not really the issue here. The elites who want to control are only interested in controlling the distribution of wealth. Those who have get more, those who don't get anything.

Proposal 1: Term Limits for Senior Administration Officials

Allowing senior level officials to stay in Washington for unlimited terms prevents real change and maintains the status quo. The two major political parties tend to appoint the same small group of elites to power positions election after election. Zbigniew Brzezinski is a prime example of a lifelong Washington politician who stayed too long. I propose that all senior and cabinet positions be restricted to the same term limits as the President – two four-year terms or a total of eight years lifetime.

Proposal 2: Limit Same Group Size

While we cannot, nor should we, prevent the president from selecting appointees from any specific group, we must also recognize that diversity of opinions and perspectives are necessary to make good decisions. Too many people from the same camp, presenting the same argument can unduly pressure a weak president, and we have had many, into making a decision that benefits the few and harms the majority of citizens. For example, Richard Nixon appointed over 100 CFR members to his administration. JFK appointed 63, Carter appointed 60, Reagan appointed 75, and George H.W. Bush appointed 350 CFR and TLC members. I propose no more than one cabinet position from any foreign policy think tank, with a limit of five members total for lower level administration positions.

CONCLUSION

"If those in charge of our society - politicians, corporate executives, and owners of press and television - can dominate our ideas, they will be secure in their power. They will not need soldiers patrolling the streets. We will control ourselves."
- Howard Zinn

Historian Howard Zinn is right about power, those who have it control America through their ideas of what is right and wrong. They regulate the present and the future through finance, information, and education. The elites have been very good in drawing a thin line that divides what is real and what is not. We are given just enough independence and information (real and not-so-real) that allows us to believe that we are in control of our lives. But we are not in control, at least of the big things our forefathers wanted us to have - liberty, freedom, and justice. The elites have created financial crises, decided who gets wealthy and who doesn't, started wars, escaped criminal prosecutions, and dumbed down the population through diluted educational curriculums – all to meet the ideological whims of a few. And in many cases, the very people we have trusted to guide us are the very ones who have betrayed us. And many of our politicians don't even realize they are mere pawns in the game of control. In his book, *The New Freedom a Call for the Emancipation of the Generous Energies of a People*, Woodrow Wilson wrote the following.

"Since I entered politics, I have chiefly had men's views confided to me privately. Some of the biggest men in the United States, in the field of commerce and manufacture, are afraid of somebody, are afraid of something. They know that there is a power somewhere so organized, so subtle, so watchful, so interlocked, so complete, so pervasive, that they had better not speak above their breath when they speak in condemnation of it."

Wilson was not alone in his warning about an organized secret partnership. Former New York City Mayor John F. Hylan gave an interview to the New York Times (December 10, 1922) reaffirming Wilson's fears. Hylan said:

"One of the most astounding facts about our American life is that the wealth and property of the country and the control of the machinery of government in the hands of less than two percent of the inhabitants. That is to say, a small group of excessively wealthy individuals, members of the republican and Democratic Parties alike, have,

through the exercise of powerful, sinister and, too often, unlawful influence, usurped the Government and seized public property on such wholesale scale that they have become the virtual dictators of the destinies of more than 110,000,000 people."

"A small group of international bankers and money lenders, public utility exploiters and tariff beneficiaries, have actually dictated nominations for offices up to the presidency. They have placed the slickest, cleverest and most cunning manipulators in official positions, even in the minor posts, where they could be of service when called upon by the invisible power, which, utterly devoid of all humanity, seeks but to wallow in riches."

Those leaders are just a few who acknowledged that an unseen, or invisible government is the ruling power of the United States. Presidents John F. Kennedy, Dwight D. Eisenhower, and Teddy Roosevelt are also on record admitting the existence of a powerful and unwanted shadow government that is free of all checks and balances.

George Carlin was right. We are controlled. What we think, what we are taught, what we are paid for our work, when and where we go to war, and who wins political office have all been staged by men and women we have never heard of. The American consciousness has been organized in relation to the interests of those who control. Changing the

Conclusion

controllers should be America's number one priority. As Mark Twain once wrote, *"Politicians and diapers must be changed often, and for the same reason."* Even when the diaper is not full, it soon will be. The longer politicians stay in office, the more likely they will be beholding to the invisible powers. Maybe changing politicians often won't eliminate all shadows, but it will cost the elites a lot more money grooming, electing, and controlling short-term politicians. Buying after-office silence will cost even more.

[1] Gallup. 75% in U.S. See Widespread Government Corruption.September 19, 2015

[2] Center for a New American Dream. New American Dream Survey 2014.

[3] Pew Research Center. The Rising Cost of Not Going to College. 2014

[4] OMB. "FEDERAL BORROWING AND DEBT." 2015.

[5] Lundberg, Ferdinand. Americas Sixty Families. New York: Vanguard Press, 1937.

[6] Charles A. Lindbergh, Sr. The Economic Pinch. Reprinted by Noontide Press, December 1968, 1923.

[7] IBID

[8] Pettinger, Tejvan. What caused the Wall Street Crash of 1929? 5 November 2012. EconomicsHelp.org.

[9] Prins, Nomi. All the Presidents' Bankers: The Hidden Alliances that Drive American Power. New York City: Nation Books, April 8, 2014.

[10] Nelson, Edward. "Milton Friedman and the Federal Reserve Chairs, 1951–1979." October 23, 2013.

[11] Congressional Oversight Panel. The AIG Rescue, Its Impact on Markets, and the Government's Exit Strategy. Washington, D.C. June 10, 2010.

[12] IBID

[13] Mukunda, Gautam. "The Price of Wall Street's Power." Harvard Business Review (June 2014).

[14] IBID

[15] Davis, Gerald F. How the Nike Model Killed the American Corporation And How Massive Outsourcing Changed Everything. June 7, 2016. B Media.

[16] Christensen, Clayton. Alton, Richard. Rising, Curtis. Waldeck, Andrew. The Big Idea: The New M&A Playbook. Harvard Business Review. March 2011.

Bibliography

17 Prins, Nomi. All the Presidents' Bankers: The Hidden Alliances that Drive American Power. New York City: Nation Books, April 8, 2014.

18 IBID

19 OpenSecrets.org: Center for Responsive Politics. n.d. January 18, 2017.

20 IBID

21 Connaughton, Jeff. The Payoff: Why Wall Street Always Wins. Westport, CT: Prospecta Press, 2012.

22 Eric Lipton, Ben Protess. Banks' Lobbyists Help in Drafting Financial Bills. 23 May 2013.

23 Steven Mufson, Tom Hamburger. "Jamie Dimon himself called to urge support for the derivatives rule in the spending bill." 11 December 2014. Washington Post.

24 The World's 50 Safest Banks 2016.Global Finance. September 8, 2016.

25 Dickler, Jessica. "College grads enjoy the best job market in years." May 17, 2016.

26 Pursuit of relevance: How higher education remains viable in today's dynamic world. IBM Institute for Business Value. 2015.

27 Bridge That Gap: Analyzing the Student Skill Index. Chegg. August 2013.

28 Board, College. "Average Published Undergraduate Charges by Sector, 2016-17." n.d.

29 Student Loan Hero. "A Look at the Shocking Student Loan Debt Statistics for 2017."

30 Smith, Jacquelyn. The Jobs with the Brightest Future. Forbes. February 2012.

31 Camera, Lauren. "High School Seniors Aren't College-Ready." U.S. News and World Report 27 April 2016.

32 Lake, Rebecca. "Shocking Facts: 23 Statistics on Illiteracy in America." May 12, 2016.

33 Center, National Student Clearinghouse Research. "Completing College: A National View of Student Attainment Rates – Fall 2010 Cohort." December 2016.

34 Carlin, George. "Who Really Controls America." 2008.

35 Spring, Joel. The American School 1642 - 2000. The American School 1642 - 2000, July 7, 2001.

[36] Association, American Historical. Report of the Commission on the Social Studies in 1934. Charles Scribner's and Sons, 1934.

[37] Iserbyt, Charlotte Thomson. The Deliberate Dumbing Down of America. 1999.

[38] Hart, Shane Vander. "Kansas House Education Committee Votes to Repeal Common Core." Truth in American Education. February 23, 2016

[39] U.S. Department Of Education: Information Security Review. Full House Committee on Oversight and Government Reform. Hearing Date: November 17, 2015

[40] Statistics, U.S Bureau of Labor. "Monthly Labor Review: Occupational Employment Projections to 2022." 2013.

[41] U.S. Census Bureau, American Community Survey, U.S. Department of Labor. n.d.

[42] Farkas, Steve and Duffett, Ann. Cracks in the Ivory Tower? Thomas B. Fordham Institute. 2010.

[43] Studying Teacher Education: The Report of the AERA Panel on Research and Teacher Education. 2009

[44] Gallup-Purdue Index Report 2015

[45] The Rewarding Work of Turning Talents into Strengths. Gallup. January 24 2017.

[46] Gallup-Purdue Index Report 2016

[47] Lake, Rebecca. Shocking Facts: 23 Statistics on Illiteracy in America. May 12, 2016.

[48] (National Institute of Child Health and Human Development. National Reading Panel Report. 2000

[49] Greenberg, Juli, Walsh, Kate, and McKee, Arthur. 2014 Teacher Prep Review. A Review of the Nation's Teacher Preparation Programs. National Council on Teacher Quality. February 2015.

[50] Quigley, Carroll. The Anglo-American Establishment. 1981

[51] The Trilateral Commission. http://trilateral.org/page/3/about-trilateral

[52] Jefferson, Thomas. In the debate over the Re-charter of the Bank Bill (1809).

[53] Diamond, Chris. The History of Money and Banking No One Ever Told You: Economic History Report. 2014.

[54] Epperson, Ralph. The Unseen Hand. 1985.

Bibliography

55 Association for Diplomatic Studies and Training. The Marshall Plan – The Europeans Did the Job Themselves. Interview by Charles Stuart Kennedy in 1996.

56 IBID

57 Emmott, Bill. Present at the creation. The Economist. June 27, 2002.

58 Pentagon Papers. United States – Vietnam Relations 1940-1950.

59 IBID.

60 IBID.

61 Tonkin Gulf Intelligence Skewed According to Official History and Intercepts. National Security Archive. Electronic Briefing Book No. 132. 2005.

62 Wise, David. The Politics of Lying: Government Deception, Secrecy and Power. 1973.

63 Pentagon Papers

64 University of Virginia. Miller Center. Lyndon B. Johnson: Foreign Affairs

65 Domhof, William. G. The Council on Foreign Relations and the Grand Area: Case Studies on the Origins of the IMF and the Vietnam War. Class, Race and Corporate Power. 2014

66 FarrelL John, A. Nixon's Vietnam Treachery. New York Times. December 31, 2016.

67 Witcover, Jules. The Dynasty That Almost Wasn't. Politico Magazine. September 15, 2015.

68 Baker, Russ. Bush Angle To Reagan Shooting Still Unresolved As Hinckley Walks. Who.What.Why. August 16, 2016

69 Cganemccalla. How The CIA Helped Create Osama Bin Laden. NEWSONE.

70 Blum, William. The Historical US Support for al-Qaeda. Foreign Policy Journal. Jan 10, 2014.

71 Gibbs, David N. The Brzezinski Interview with Le Nouvel Observateur (1998). University of Arizona.

72 Brzezinski, Zbigniew. Toward a Global Realignment. The American Interest. August 17, 2016.

73 UNCLASSIFIED U.S. Department of State Case No. F-2014-20439 Doc No. C05779612 Date: 12/31/2015. Email sent on Saturday, April 2, 2011 10:44 PM from Sidney Blumenthal to Hilary Clinton. Subject: France's client & Q's gold.

74 Phillips, Peter. Censored 2010: The Top 25 Censored Stories of 2008-09. 2009

75 Bush, George. H.W. and Scowcroft, Bren. A World Transformed. Knopf, 1998.

76 Leung, Rebecca. Bush Sought 'Way' To Invade Iraq? O'Neill Tells '60 Minutes' Iraq Was 'Topic A' 8 Months Before 9-11.60 Minutes. January 9, 2004.

77 Battle, Joyce. The Iraq War -- Part I: The U.S. Prepares for Conflict, 2001. National Security Archive Electronic Briefing Book No. 326. Posted - September 22, 2010.

Made in the USA
Coppell, TX
02 June 2020

26831986R00103